AF060253

Coffee in Yemen
A Practical Guide

J. Brian D. Robinson

Rural Development Project Al-Mahwit Province

KLAUS SCHWARZ VERLAG • BERLIN • 1993

Copyright: © 1993

Deutsche Gesellschaft für Technische Zusammenarbeit (GTZ) GmbH
Dag-Hammarskjöld-Weg 1+2,
W-6236 Eschborn 1
Federal Republic of Germany

ISBN 3-87997-214-1
Layout and Typesetting:
Fritz Piepenburg

Photos:
J. Brian D. Robinson, Ernst Schröder, Fritz Piepenburg

Drawings:
Andrea Selim

Colour Separation:
Schwangart Repro, Kaufbeuren, Federal Republic of Germany

Printing:
HORIZONS FOR PRINTING & PUBLISHING
TEL:612844 P.O BOX:12503

Special thanks are extended to the Yemeni staff of the Rural Development Project Al-Mahwit Province (RDPM), in particular Mr. Abdul Jabbar, for their cooperation and field assistance in the process of producing this manual.

FOREWORD

This practical guide to arabica coffee growing has been written primarily for Coffee Advisory staff, progressive coffee growers and as a teaching or training manual.

The objectives have been to improve productivity per unit area and to improve the quality of the green bean whilst maintaining the health and vigour of the commercial arabica coffee trees.

Recognised and successful international techniques based upon research work done in many leading producer countries have been considered: selected practices have been adapted and adjusted for the very unique growing conditions present in the highlands of the Yemen Arab Republic. They were arrived at after field observations of the current methods practised by farmers during field tours in the northern parts of the country.

A more usual and logical procedure would be for new production techniques to be examined under controlled conditions within a programme of adaptive research at a national level. Such a programme would examine and assess these techniques against traditional methods in a critical manner. In the absence of a national coffee research structure this approach is not possible at the present time.

Such comparisons of field techniques may only be made at present by small scale demonstration on individual farmer's coffee trees when more advanced growers are prepared to co-operate. However, improved seedling production techniques can be adopted in central nurseries.

Establishing small field demonstrations on a few farmer-trees is not easy to implement because in general, coffee growers will not permit visiting technical staff to do anything more than look, comment and discuss coffee problems and growing methods.

J. Brian D. Robinson
Coffee Specialist

Contents

FOREWORD iii

1. **INTRODUCTION** 1

2. **THE ARABICA COFFEE TREE, YEMEN VARIETIES AND SEED PREPARATION.** 3
   The Tree 3
   Coffee Varieties 7
   Seed Preparation 8

3. **ENVIRONMENTAL CONDITIONS** 11
   Climate 11
   Soil 12

4. **COFFEE NURSERY METHODS AND SEEDLING PRODUCTION** 15
   Problems 15
   General Nursery Techniques 16
   Small Farmer Nurseries 19
   Large or Central Nurseries 20

5. **FIELD PLANTING** 25
   Problems 25
   Spacing 25
   Interplanting 26
   Holing 27
   Transplanting 27

6. **PRUNING** 31
   The Survival of a Healthy Coffee Tree 31
   Problems 32
   Pruning Methods 32

7. WEEDING AND INTERCROPPING 43
Weed control 43
Intercropping 44

8. SHADE AND SHELTER 45

9. IRRIGATION, WATER USE AND MULCHING 51
Irrigation 51
Water Use 52
Mulching with Stones 53

10. MANURE AND FERTILISER 57
Key to Mineral Deficiency or Imbalance Symptoms ... 57
Organic Manure 61
Fertilisers 61

11. PHYSIOLOGICAL AND OTHER DISORDERS 65
Genetic Effects 65
Climatic Effects 65
Overbearing Dieback amd Debility Syndrome 68

12. DISEASES AND PESTS 71
Diseases 71
Pests 74

13. HARVESTING AND PROCESSING 79
Picking 79
Drying 80
Hulling 81
Roasting 82

14. GENERAL OBSERVATIONS 83
Timeliness and the Coffee Calendar 83
Irrigation Pattern and Water Use 83
Root System Development and Early Cropping Levels ... 84
Pest Control 84
Coffee Research 86

REFERENCES 87

List of Figures

Figure 1: The Coffee Tree 4

Figure 2: Section of a Coffee Cherry 6

Figure 3: Germination Bed, Nursery Bed and Coffee Seedlings 18

Figure 4: Planting Hole, Nursery and Seedlings Planted Out 31

Figure 5: Early Pruning of Young Coffee Trees 34

Figure 6: Pruning Single and Multiple Stem 38

Figure 7: Rejuvenation/Regeneration of Old Coffee Trees 39

Figure 8: Possible Shapes of Shade Trees 48

Figure 9: Coffee Pests 73

Figure 10: Outline Coffee Calendar 85

1. INTRODUCTION

Arabica coffee production in the Republic of Yemen (ROY) occupies a unique position in the history of this crop. It is generally agreed that while natural, wild arabica coffee was harvested from underneath forest tree cover in Ethiopia, deliberate, formal cultivation of this crop was first done in the Republic of Yemen with seed brought across the Red Sea possibly from the Harar area of Ethiopia. Although exact dates are not known, it is probable that formal cultivation commenced in the 1300's AD and nowhere else until the 1600's AD. With respect to the southern parts of the country arabica coffee is said to have been the first systematic terrace cropping in the country (1, 2).

There are two principal sites for cultivation in the country. These are coffee grown on hillside terraces (broad-based, narrow-based and step-terraces) and in the Wadi bottoms. Most of the coffee grown is irrigated to a greater or lesser degree i.e. there is irrigated coffee, seasonally irrigated coffee and coffee that receives emergency irrigation at times in what is referred to as rainfed coffee.

Since coffee is agriculturally a very forgiving crop it is not surprising that for several of the field operations there are often alternative acceptable 'best' practices. There are certain basic guidelines fundamental to the growing of good trees and the economic production of quality beans. In summary these are:

i) Selection of the best available site with reference to soil depth, drainage and fertility, slope, altitude with respect to rainfall, temperature range, exposure to desiccating winds and a convenient source of water for irrigation.

ii) The production of good quality coffee seedlings of the right age and size at the correct time for planting out in the field. Choice of an appropriate coffee variety or varieties will also be significant.

iii) Accurate and correct preparation and planting of the site. This implies accurate lining-out of planting sites, excavation of proper planting holes, manuring the in-fill, careful lifting of the seedlings (if not grown in polypots) and correct transplanting techniques.

iv) Timely establishment of shade trees, temporary or permanent and of windbreak trees where necessary.

v) Effective weed control at all times particularly grass weed growing close to the coffee.

vi) Adoption and timely application of a regular and standardised pruning system.
vii) Avoidance of overbearing by the coffee at all times.
viii) Regular and correct application of organic manure.
ix) Timely control of any serious outbreak of pests or disease.
x) A careful and high standard of harvesting and processing the ripe coffee cherry.
xi) Clean and safe storage of dried cherry or green bean.
xii) The economical management of irrigation water in association with soil mulch cover.

The production of quality arabica coffee grown in the Republic of Yemen can be improved. The main areas in need of general improvement are seedling quality, transplanting techniques, pruning and handling, irrigation water management with mulching, harvesting and processing.

The major field problems observed in the coffee are iron (deficiency) chlorosis, lack of pruning and the very serious overbearing/debility syndrome condition of many trees.

Since arabica coffee is a long-term tree crop, good management in the field is a long-term need. Under Yemeni conditions a grower should be actively concerned with the current season's crop production and tree condition plus activities needed to achieve targeted production at least in the following year and preferably two years.

Finally, there is an appreciable consumer demand in some developed countries for organically-produced, natural foods and drinks; coffee is no exception and in general, Yemeni coffee produced by the small scale farmer is of this category. Careful thought and great care are needed in respect of any future consideration for the use of modern agricultural chemicals that could change this situation. Generally speaking and largely because of the unique climatic conditions for coffee growing, serious pest and disease outbreaks have been rare and/or short lived. There is another very important reason for the need of care in the future with synthetic agricultural chemicals: this is the unique use of the coffee cherry skins to prepare the drink Gishr. Harmful chemical residues from some of the materials currently available could accumulate in the cherry skins from trees treated for the control of pests and diseases .

2. THE ARABICA COFFEE TREE, YEMEN VARIETIES AND SEED PREPARATION

The Tree

In its country of origin (Ethiopia and Southern Sudan) arabica coffee (*Coffea arabica*) is a small understorey tree of variable height to about 9 m tall, growing in the upland forests. A representation of a young, unpruned coffee tree is shown in Figure 1 with the names of the vegetative and root system parts clearly labelled (3).

The root system of arabica coffee is often modified from this diagrammatic form by soil and cultural conditions. In Kenya for example, a small mature tree will root to a depth of 3 m under natural rainfall conditions whereas in the central highlands of Colombia where rainfall is both higher and more regularly distributed, rooting to a depth of about 1 m is usual. In Yemen it is the practice of irrigation that will modify root distribution along with a lack of adequate soil depth. The rooting form will have a shorter, shallower taproot with a denser and more widespread development of the lateral root system (4).

Five types of root have been described and are shown in Figure 1:

i) The tap root is a stout central root growing vertically downwards into the soil to a variable depth depending upon soil texture, soil drainage, total annual rainfall and its distribution and the application of a regular irrigation water regime. As a recognisable unit it rarely extends below 0.5 to 1 m and its main functions are to anchor the tree in the ground and it is the central frame of the root system.

ii) Axial roots often originate in the forking of the tap root where this has been cut or damaged. They may be lateral roots that have turned downwards to form "droppers", a change that frequently occurs when the tap root is severely damaged. There are generally 4 - 8 axial roots developed. They are capable of deep penetration (2 - 3 m) in permeable free draining soil and where conditions are seasonally dry in the top metre or more.

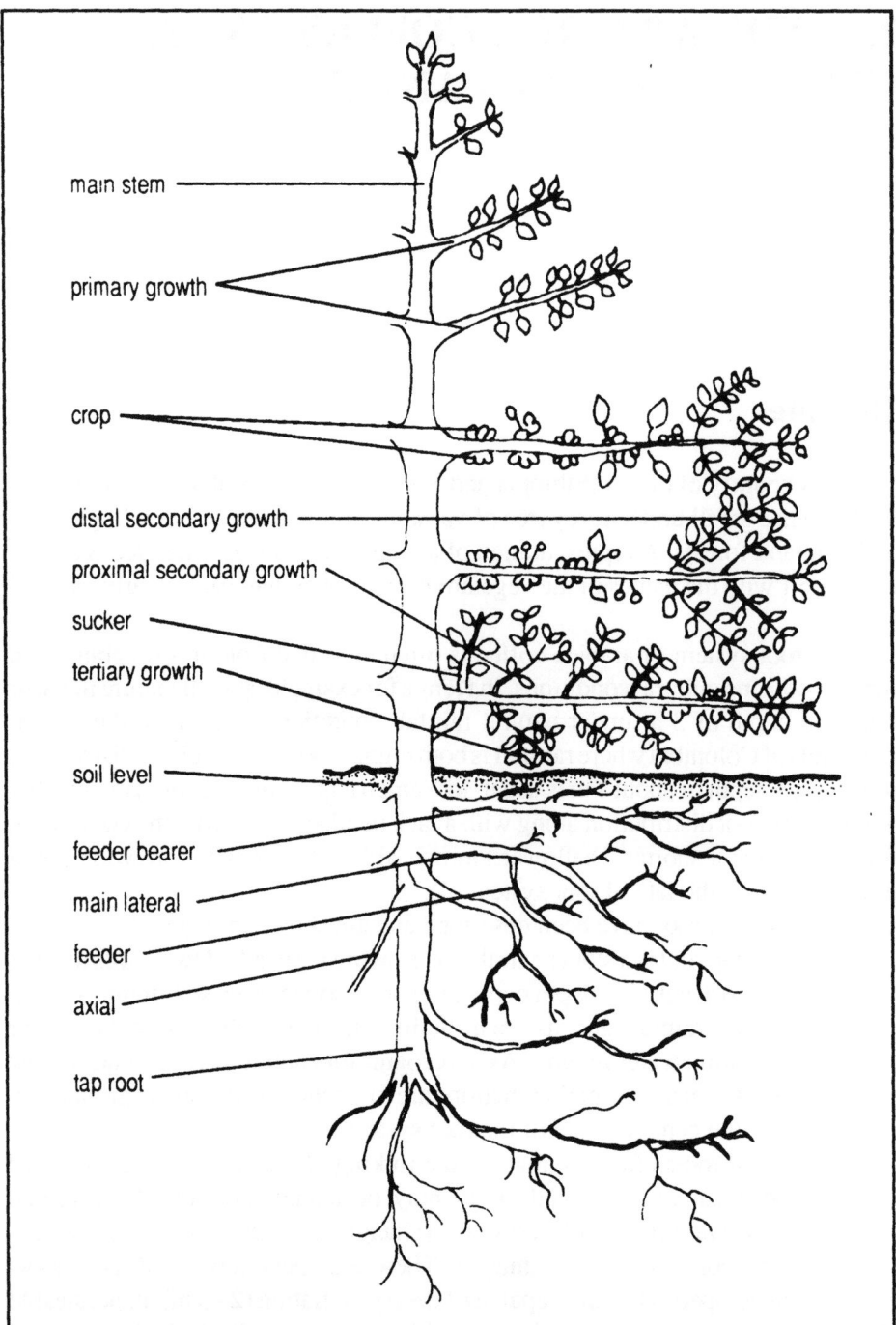

Figure 1: The Coffee Tree

iii) Lateral roots may be either surface plate-roots growing outwards horizontally and parallel to the soil surface 2 m deep or less depending upon planting density, configuration, soil type and soil moisture conditions. Where the coffee tree develops a deep root system a second type of lateral root that is not in the surface plate may arise deeper within the soil profile. It spreads out evenly in the soil and branches out in all planes.

iv) Feeder-bearer roots are of varying length, generally evenly distributed about every 3 cm along the permanent lateral roots.

v) Feeder roots are carried uniformly on the feeder-bearers at all depths but tend to be more numerous in the surface soil where the structure is more friable.

The main stem and branches comprise a central dominant vertical stem with horizontal primary lateral branches arising from it in pairs, opposite each other. The lateral buds are always single and if a primary branch dies or is cut off it is not replaced. On the primaries, paired secondary lateral branches develop and these will branch further to form tertiary and subsequently quaternary lateral branches largely spread in an horizontal place at right angles to the central stem. The weight of foliage and fruit causes the branch to droop to a degree that varies with the cultivar. All these except quaternary lateral branches are illustrated in Figure 1.

Suckers are upright shoots that develop from the main stem(s) particularly when the latter are cut back i.e. pruned, or bent over (Agobiada system of vertical generation). When young it is known as a sucker and it arises just below the point of attachment of a primary lateral branch. As it develops it produces horizontal lateral branches and assumes the habit of a main stem or vertical.

Secondary and tertiary branches on the primary lateral branch may develop in different positions namely (a) from the terminal bud of a strong primary often a considerable distance from its point of origin on the main stem. The development of these distal sub-laterals at the same time as primary branch extension is taking place provides additional leaf area and extra bearing wood for the following year; (b) proximal sub-laterals may develop near the main stem(s) (or verticals) from nodes on a primary or secondary lateral usually in the season following a heavy crop on the primary branch.

Leaves occur in opposite pairs along the side of branches; young leaves may be coloured either light green or bronze. Where the bronze colour is present it is visible only at a certain stage of leaf development, usually when young. It develops in young leaves and then gradually fades with maturation leaving the adult leaf entirely green. While mature leaves vary in size according to variety, season, location, shade presence and nutritional status they are usually 7-15 cm long, lanceolate, ribbed and they shine with a wax covering.

Flowers can be borne on all forms of lateral branches and buds are present in series in the leaf axis.

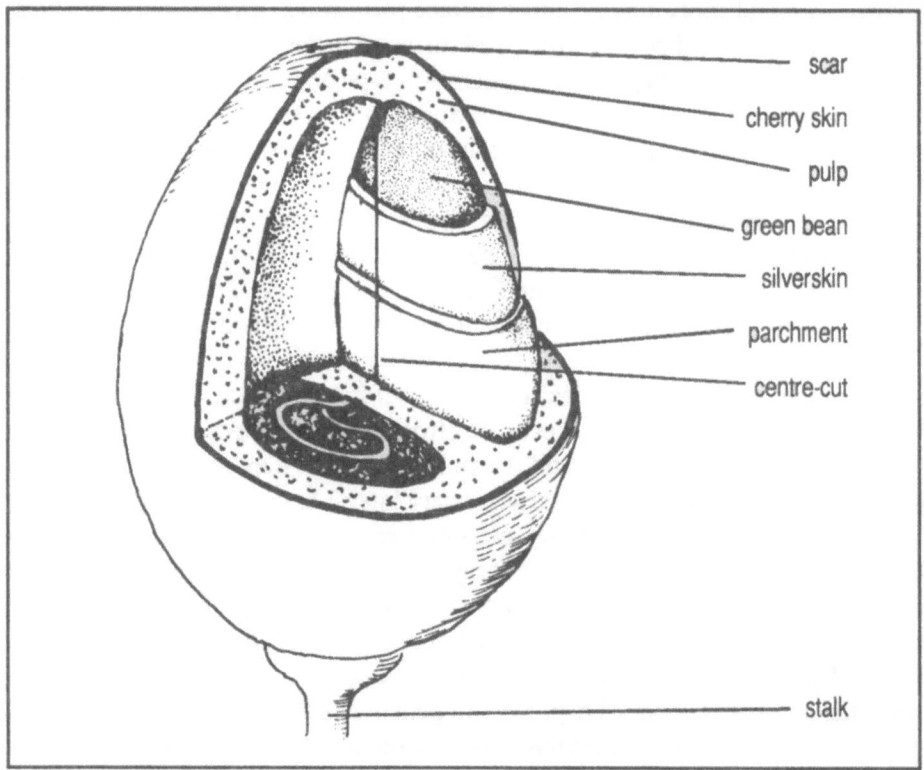

Figure 2: Section of a Coffee Cherry

Flower buds emerge just as inflorescences numbering 2 - 6 in each axil, 4 - 12 or even more at each node and each one usually consists of 4 flowers on short stalks attached to a main stalk. Numbers may vary with the variety. Each flower has a white corolla with 5 lobes, and is sweet-scented; flowering is generally triggered-off by rainfall or irrigation following a dry period during which a condition of internal water stress builds up in the tree. There are usually one or two main flowerings but a number of small subsidiary flowerings may occur and the pattern is closely related to climatic conditions and/or irrigation application. A flowering lasts for 2 - 3 days.

Arabica coffee is largely self-fertilising (>90%) and the percentage of natural pollination producing hybrids is only about 7 - 9% (Brazilian data).

The amount of fruit (cherry) set is variable and the time taken from blossoming to maturity (fully red-ripe) varies between 8 - 10 months. In warmer conditions i.e. lower altitudes, it is of a shorter time but in cooler conditions it will be longer and may exceed 11 months.

Fruit (cherry) is oval-elliptical with a short stalk and a scar at the apex. It averages about 14 mm long and 13 mm width but this varies with the variety. In harsh soil moisture and drought conditions, particularly when it is unshaded, the potential cherry size is markedly reduced. It normally contains two seeds or beans, flat on one side but may contain only one seed (peaberry) or three seeds triangular in shape (triage). The green bean is covered by the silverskin membrane which is covered in turn by a tough parchment skin. In the fresh cherry a coating of slimy mucilage covers the parchment and the beans are enclosed with a pulpy flesh and then the smooth skin. When ripe the skin colour is brilliant to dark red (Figure 2).

Coffee Varieties

The coffee varieties that are recognised in each of the main growing locations are almost certainly local farmer selections made over the centuries of cultivation. To this day there has been no serious collection, botanical description or economic study made of Yemeni varieties at the national level. History suggests that the source of coffee originated from Ethiopia, probably from one or perhaps two regions there. It is most probable that the genetic base of arabica coffee in the ROY is narrow with only limited opportunities for increasing yield potential and other desirable characteristics e.g. enhanced drought resistance, strong and deep rooting, from within the existing material.

There is a need to collect, study and evaluate the nationally available varieties thoroughly before any consideration is given to bringing in new varieties from elsewhere for careful assessment. This is the type of research project well suited to the Faculty of Agriculture of the University of Sanaa.

There is one other important coffee characteristic in addition to bean yield and quality that is peculiar to the ROY - it is the value and the use made of the dry cherry skin and mucilage or pulp for the preparation of the beverage known as Gishr.

During field tours in the Al Mahwit Province farmers identified different local varieties that they cultivated often for quite specific reasons. Desirable variety characters noted were:

i) Varieties grown primarily for their bean yield and liquor quality rather than for the yield of cherry skin + mucilage.

ii) Varieties grown primarily for their skin + mucilage quality e.g. volume and sweetness of the mucilage, rather than for the yield of bean which was important but of secondary significance.

iii) Dual purpose varieties combining the desirable characteristics of both i) and ii) above.

iv) Varieties with a short cropping season i.e. a more determinate flowering pattern.

v) Varieties with a long, extended cropping season.

vi) Semi-dwarf varieties with a bushy form making denser population planting possible and harvesting the crop easier.

vii) Yellow-ripe coloured cherry varieties.

Varieties encountered in the fields of the Al Mahwit Province are listed in Table 1. The name spelling is that which was recorded in the field initially but it is known that other spellings of the same varieties occur in different localities.

All these varieties except the semi-dwarfs, are tall arabica coffees.

Yemeni Arabica Coffee Varieties Noted Growing in Al Mahwit

Variety Name	Variety Characteristic
Adeni	Grown for both bean and cherry skin
Adeni Bayat	Yellow-ripe cherry colour, low yield of high quality bean
Burai	Grown for the bean principally
Benan	Semi-dwarf coffee
Benan Bayat	Semi-dwarf coffee with yellow-ripe cherry colour
Touffahai	Grown for the bean principally
Sawat	Semi-dwarf with larger leaves than Benan. Tree has a very round shape i.e. bushy.
Dawairy	Grown for the bean principally
Shabraque	?
Dohairj	Grown for the bean principally
Dohairi	Said to possess some degree of drought resistance

Seed Preparation

Careful attention to the preparation of good quality seed is not very apparent though standards are variable.

It is not satisfactory to use any old unsorted green bean or dried cherry (*Bun*) coffee for seed and good quality seed must be carefully prepared. Generally speaking for a particular coffee variety, large 'A' grade quality beans (not peaberries, triage or 'elephant' beans) have the potential to produce strong seedlings. Beans of different coffee varieties should not be mixed-up together. Dried cherry is not a good source of seed since the size of the bean is unknown and sowing seed singly is not possible.

Seed should only be taken from carefully selected, fully red-ripe cherries and never from green or yellow/orange coloured cherry (from a red-fruited coffee variety) which is under-ripe or droughted, nor from over-ripe or black cherries.

Germination percentage will be optimum when prepared from freshly picked, fully ripe cherry, hand-pulped (skin removed by hand) within 24 hours of picking and then sown fresh. However, time of sowing must be related to the optimum time for seedling transplanting to the field and this may necessitate storing seed before sowing.

Seed for storage should be hand-pulped fresh cherry, graded by eye for even, average size, rolled in cold wood ash (fire ash) and dried in a single layer in the shade, never in direct sunlight. When dry the ash-covered seed may be stored in a cool, shaded corner in a coarse woven cloth bag or sack; never store in a polythene bag.

Seed carefully prepared and stored in this manner should retain a germination percentage of 80% or higher over a period of 3 - 4 months or even longer.

Note:
a) Unusually large or small beans should be discarded from the seed sample.
b) If the seed is hulled to the green bean stage all damaged and black beans should be discarded.
c) Immediately after hand-pulping the ripe cherry for seed production the slimy (mucilage covered) parchment beans should be placed in a bowl, basin or bucket of water. Any 'light' beans that float on top must be discarded and only the sunken, heavy beans be retained as seed.

3. ENVIRONMENTAL CONDITIONS

Climate

It is fair to describe in general terms the climate in which arabica coffee is grown in the ROY as very variable and harsh.

Optimum conditions for arabica coffee production have been summarised (5) as 15.5 - 24°C mean annual minimum and maximum temperatures. Day temperatures should not exceed 30 - 35°C and night temperatures should not fall below 7 - 10°C for any appreciable length of time. The diurnal (daily) temperature ranges should not exceed 19°C. Total rainfall for rainfed coffee production should be of the order of 1500 - 1900 mm with either one (unimodal rainfall distribution) or two (bimodal rainfall distributions) dry periods not exceeding 2 - 3 months duration.

Persistent wind particularly if it is of a dry desiccating nature and the occurrence of hail storms, are adverse to coffee growing.

The more suitable the climatic conditions are, the easier it will be to grow and manage the crop to produce good economic yields of high quality coffee.

Because of the variable and rugged topography, climatic conditions are very variable in many of the coffee growing areas. Rainfall totals are generally low and very variable. Persistent winds and occasional hail storms (albeit of short duration) occur and under both wadi and upland terrace conditions the aspect (directional orientation) of the coffee land can be a factor of considerable significance.

Detailed and reliable climatic records for the coffee growing areas are not available. But, in very general terms, there is usually a 5 - 6 month hot dry season and a 5 - 6 month wet season: with some regional variation the dry season extends from September/October to February/March and the wet season from March/April to August/September but June is frequently a dry month. Rainfall totals can be very variable and the number of months in which effective rainfall is received varies widely with local topographic variations.

It has been reported for the Al Mahwit Province that the average rainfall is of the order of 500 mm with an average range of 400 - 900 mm (6). The FAO (1975) report gives rainfall data for the Taiz region (1,350 m asl) of mean = 527 mm and an annual range 277 - 722 mm over a 5 year period, nearly a three-fold variation (7).

A further point of significance about rainfall concerns the intensity of downfall. Very heavy showers are frequent and run-off can be a serious factor preventing moisture take-up by the soil.

Little or no detailed temperature information is available but the occurrence of the physiological disorders on the coffee, particularly young trees, of Hot and Cold symptoms (Crinkle Leaf) attributed to wide diurnal temperature variation indicates an adverse range of daily temperature at some stage in the season. Equally, the occurrence of intermittent chlorosis on leaf pairs resulting from particularly low night temperatures can be observed occasionally and is said to develop following nights when frosts occur at higher altitudes i.e. arising from particularly low night time temperature conditions. Both these conditions are described with photographs in references (8), (9) and in (10). Diurnal temperature ranges in wadi/valley bottoms can be very wide, attributable to the downward movements of cold air during the night-time.

In some areas e.g. parts of the Hufash area in Al Mahwit Province, cloud cover during the day time in the dry season is a beneficial climatic condition. It reduces day time temperatures and hence evapotranspiration water losses and decreases the low night-time temperatures thus reducing the otherwise overly wide diurnal temperature range.

Soil

While arabica coffee will grow over a wide range of soil texture and of soil fertility, the more suitable these conditions are the easier it is to grow good coffee trees. Arabica coffee will not thrive in poorly drained or shallow soil (particularly if rainfed) without a great deal of extra input e.g. drainage, irrigation, mulching, inorganic manure etc. Preferably the soil should be a friable loam or lateritic clay with a minimum depth of 1.5 - 2.0 m. This depth requirement may be less with a high, evenly distributed rainfall or where a careful, regulated system of irrigation is practised when rainfall is limiting, and in the presence of a surface mulch to reduce evaporative water loss. Arabica coffee prefers acid soil pH conditions, ideally 5.2 - 6.0 (1:1, soil to water ratio method) or 4.4 - 5.8 (1:2.5, soil to M/100 CaC_{12} ratio method) but it is widely grown over a pH range of 4.4 - 6.8 (1:1, soil to water ratio method). The soil should be well supplied with exchangeable base nutrients i.e. potassium and magnesium in particular; at high pH levels (alkaline, > pH 7.0) iron and sometimes manganese may be seriously limiting to both vegetative growth and quality crop production. A sustained and adequate supply of nitrogen from the soil is necessary for good crop production.

The coffee soils seen in the field were all dominated physically by their fine sand and silt contents often with a high stone content also. Texture varied from sands through sandy silts and silty sands to sandy silt loams and silty loams. In many instances texture has developed because of irrigation water suspensions carried into the crop, often over centuries of irrigation. This is a situation most strongly relating to the use of hill run-off waters and wadi waters for irrigation. The salt content of irrigation waters applied over generations also largely accounts for the high (alkaline) soil pH values generally >7.0 - 8.5. These soils particularly the lighter textured types, often have a low soil organic matter content and the available plant water holding capacity is frequently low particularly on some of the lighter soil types.

In conclusion, the difficult and often harsh environmental conditions for coffee cultivation are a reflection of a difficult climate, often adverse physical and chemical soil conditions and difficult topographical conditions particularly on steeper hillside terraces.

4. COFFEE NURSERY METHODS AND SEEDLING PRODUCTION

Problems

A good quality coffee seedling is the first stage in growing healthy and high yielding coffee trees. In general terms the quality of farmer-grown seedlings is less than satisfactory and the general techniques used in large central nurseries are often not the best proven methods.

Farmer nurseries are generally small in area, densely spaced as the result of broadcasting seed or even whole cherry over the surface with little regard for an adequate spacing. Seedlings are often raised like this to the age of transplanting into the field. The nursery bed is sunken i.e. a basin, or a basin is formed by planting on the flat and raising the soil around the perimeter. Watering is by flooding sometimes from a high pressure pipe resulting in soil movement that raises the soil level around the seedling stems producing a very adverse "deep planting" effect. Shade is usually provided by growing trees, or rock overhang or by wire mesh, and is permanent so that there is seldom any 'hardening off' process of the seedlings by progressive reduction in shade cover. Careless lifting for bare-root transplanting often gives broken tap roots and generally destroys a high proportion of the young tender lateral roots. Farmers do generally give the nursery bed-soil a dressing of manure before sowing the seed (Plates 1,2).

In large central nurseries seedlings raised in a germination bed are transplanted into polypots (black diothene plastic pots). Some common faults observed were:
i) The use of unselected seed i.e. no removal of lights, no size grading
ii) Seed broadcast not hand-sown at a specific spacing, in either sunken or flat germination beds (Plate 1).
iii) No specific treatment applied to correct nitrogen or iron deficiency in the seedlings. These conditions stunt growth (Plates 3, 4 and 5).
iv) Transplanting from the germination beds to polypots is carried out at the 2 to 4 true leaf stage. This is far too late and accounts for a great deal of early root damage (Plates 6, 7).

v) While the formula for the potting soil is theoretically correct the resulting mixture lacked texture and compacts badly. The sand used is usually too fine and the quantity of powdery organic manure too little.
vi) Potted seedlings are generally raised in sunken beds with a cement stone surround without drainage. In very wet weather or with overwatering, temporary waterlogging occurs limiting root development and top growth (Plates 5, 8).
vii) Watering the germination beds and polypot beds in dry weather is usually done with irrigation hose (open ended) at high pressure. This frequently washes the potting mixture out of the pots leaving the seedlings to develop in a 2/3 to 1/2 filled polypot only. This restricts root development severely and encourages deep rooting below the pot in the soil beneath (Plate 8).
viii) As a result of (vii) when the polypot seedlings are taken out into the field the root growth below the bottom of the pot is cut off, effectively removing a significant portion of the system and leaving a comparatively large top supported by an inadequate root system. Such seedlings are slow to grow away and are very drought susceptible. This situation could delay production of the first small crop by a season.
ix) Shade cover is usually plastic mesh on a metal frame. It is not practicable to permanently reduce shade cover progressively through three stages to zero and so harden the seedlings off before they go out into the field.
x) Where seedlings are provided to farmers in the bare-root form to facilitate transport it is essential that they are treated adequately to prevent excessive drying out, serious wilting or death before the transplanting operation is completed.

An improvement in nursery standards does not necessarily require large, expensive financial input, whether for the small farmer or the larger central nursery. Recommended basic methods are as described.

General Nursery Techniques

i) Sow individual, carefully selected and prepared coffee seed (refer Chapter 2).
ii) Do not broadcast-sow coffee seed in a random manner; plant carefully at a specific spacing.
iii) Sow seed flat side down at a depth of 1.25 cm in either beds or polypots (Figure 3).

iv) Germination and nursery beds should be raised 10 - 15 cm above the surrounding soil area to prevent waterlogging and facilitate good root development (Figure 3). Sunken beds, nursery beds or polypot beds should not be sunk (basin shaped). However, polypots can be set out on a flat land surface.

v) Seed germination can be speeded up by (a) soaking dried seed in water for 24 hours or (b) removing the parchment cover by hand prior to sowing. This latter method reduces the normal germination time of 6 - 10 weeks (40 - 50 days in ROY) by 50% or more.

vi) Transplanting from germination beds should be carried out at the "Helmet" or "Butterfly" stages of growth but never later i.e. after the production of one or two true-leaf pairs as is generally practised now (Plate 6, Figure 3).

vii) Use a simple wooden planting stick to lift small seedlings from the germination bed, to make the planting hole in the permanent bed or polypot and to firm the soil around the transplanted seedlings (Figure 3).

viii) Never damage or bend the tap root when transplanting the coffee seedling.

ix) Never deep-plant the coffee seedling i.e. bury the seedling stem below the original level in the germination bed.

x) Depending upon nursery care and conditions strong seedlings should take between 8 - 11 months to develop, usually 9 - 10 months should be sufficient time to produce a polypot seedling which is 25 - 30 cm tall with maturing bark on the main stem to a height of about 10 cm and with one or two pairs of lateral branches.

xi) Coffee seedlings must be carefully and gradually hardened-off while in the nursery. This is achieved by removing permanently the shade cover in three distinct stages until they are completely unshaded. Transplanting shade-covered seedlings from the nursery into the field under open, unshaded conditions is a poor planting practice unless temporary shade is provided in the field.

Figure 3 contains diagrams of a raised germination bed, a raised nursery bed, seed sowing, transplanting stages of seedling growth (see also Plate 6) and the transplanting stick referred to.

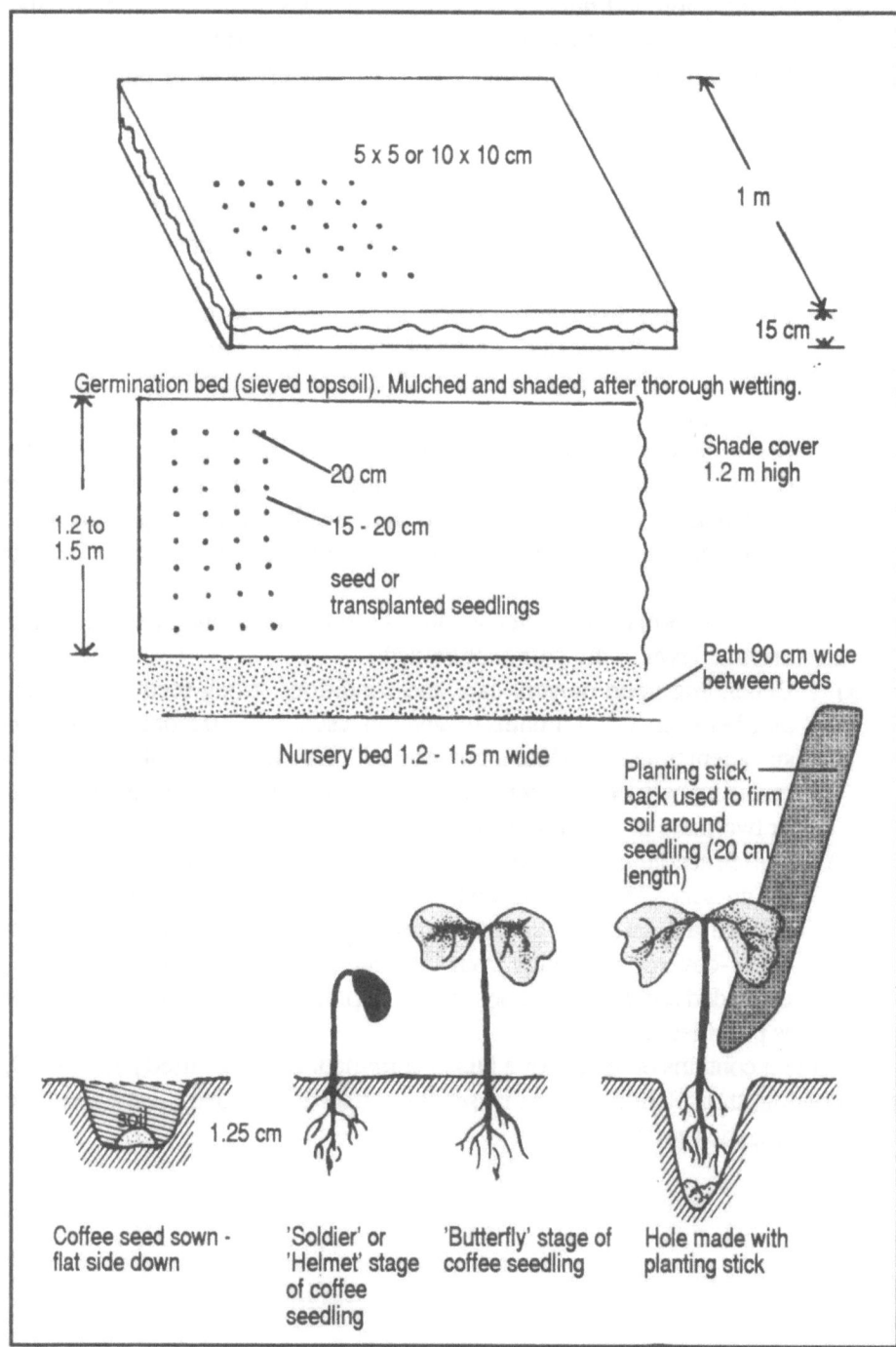

Figure 3: Germination Bed, Nursery Bed and Coffee Seedlings

Small Farmer Nurseries

As seems to be the general situation, it is assumed that a small farmer will sow his coffee seed on a single site to produce his own seedlings. He will not use a germination bed and transplant to a nursery bed or into polypots.

i) The small nursery bed should be raised above the surrounding ground level by 10 - 15 cm with topsoil plus manure.

ii) Fine, dry mature animal manure should be mixed thoroughly with the topsoil at a rate of 2 - 3 kg/m^2.

iii) The raised seedbed should be 1.2 to 1.5 m wide with the seeds sown at a spacing of 10 cm between seeds in the line and 10 - 15 cm between lines at a depth of 1.25 cm, flat side down.

iv) Until germination has occurred the bed should be mulched with fine grass or leaf material to sustain a moist, cool environment.

v) When the seedlings have emerged above ground, move the organic mulch to the inter- seed-line-space or if the organic material is required for other purposes e.g. animal feed, mulch the inter-seed-line-space with small stones laid close together. The more effective the mulch cover of the soil is the less frequent will be the need to water.

vi) A shade cover giving roughly 70 - 80% shade cover should be erected at least 75 cm above the seedbed e.g. sorghum stalks supported on a wooden or wire frame.

vii) Watering should be done at low pressure, sprinkled onto the bed through a plastic rose head (available in Sana'a) attached to a spout from a metal or plastic container (can) or to an irrigation hose. On no account should a high pressure hose supply be used but the operator's thumb may be applied over the pipe/hose end of a low pressure supply to create a fine, gentle spray. Do not apply water by hose with a high pressure jet. Avoid surface flood irrigation if possible.

viii) Keep the bed clean weeded and protect from animal damage.

ix) Assuming a 10 month long period in the nursery, start reducing the density of the shade cover between 5- 6 months by thinning the shade to a 50 - 60% cover; repeat the thinning further to a 25 - 30% cover after another 6 weeks and finally remove all shade cover 6 weeks later i.e. coffee seedlings are now completely unshaded.

x) When ready to carry out transplanting into the field, thoroughly wet the seedling bed; do not pull up the seedlings but dig them up with a fork or the local single-tine hoe carefully.

xi) Do not damage the lateral roots and rootlets or cut/break the tap root off. Plant out as soon after lifting as possible.

xii) If seedlings (bare-rooted after lifting) have to be transported far in hot sunny conditions wrap them in wet paper and/or wet cloth. Do not put them inside a closed plastic bag.

xiii) If it becomes necessary to retain coffee seedlings in the nursery because of surplus numbers or because the planting season is over or the weather conditions are adverse, it is possible to do this by cutting off the distal half of all the leaves on a seedling. This prevents overgrowing and weakness of the seedlings.

Large or Central Nurseries

There are four alternative methods for growing coffee seedlings in a large nursery.

i) Sowing seed directly into a raised seedling bed at a wide spacing suitable for the complete growing cycle (20 x 20 cm).

ii) Sowing seed directly into a raised germination bed for transplanting (a) into a raised seedling bed or (b) into polypots (200 gauge black diothene of lay-flat size 25 x 15 cm). Spacing in a true sand bed (7.5 cm deep) should be 2.5 x 2.5 cm; in a germination bed of topsoil and manure it should be 5 x 5 cm. The transplant spacing into a raised nursery bed is again 20 x 20 cm.

iii) Sowing seed directly into polypots full of potting compost, one seed per pot with a small back-up germination bed (raised) to cater for (say) 20% misses. Polypot seedlings are preferred because (a) the root system is neither exposed nor disturbed when transplanted, (b) seedlings can be transported over long distances safely and (c) actual transplanting can be delayed if weather conditions are unsuitable. A disadvantage is the actual transporting of seedlings over long distances compared with bare-root seedlings.

Of these alternatives, the last method of direct sowing into polypots is preferred. The principal requirements are:

i) The nursery site must have a convenient, reliable and permanent water supply. The topography should be flat or gently undulating, it should be sheltered from strong winds and should not be situated in valley bottoms or hollows into which cold air settles at night. Animals which might damage coffee seedlings e.g. goats, chickens, must be kept out of the nursery sites.

ii) The soil of the germination or seedling bed should be deep, friable, with a good organic matter content producing a fine tilth. Organic material should be incorporated into the top 15 cm of the raised bed at about 20% by volume.

iii) When growing polypot seedlings the potting mixture needs to be prepared with care. Generally a manure:sand:topsoil ratio of 1:2:3 parts is used but it is often less than satisfactory because the manure is fine, dry and well matured, the sand size is too small (< 1 mm diam.) and the topsoil texture is often dominated by its fine sand content. This mixture quickly packs down after wetting and becomes consolidated with consequent lack of aeration which inhibits root development. In this situation and with the general need for a higher nitrogen content and a lower pH value of the compost, the mixture would be more suitable if a formula of 2:2:2 parts of fine manure, coarse sand (4 - 5 mm) and topsoil were made up. The need is to maintain an open, free draining and well aerated texture in the polypot throughout the whole life of the seedling.

iv) If well rotted animal manure is not available or is in short supply, composted coffee hullings may be used as a substitute for animal manure.

v) Germination beds (1 m wide), seedling beds (1.2 - 1.5 m wide) and polypot stands (1.5 m wide) should all be orientated in an east-west direction for maximum efficiency of overhead shade.

vi) Germination and seedling beds should be raised 15 cm above the surrounding path levels. Paths between beds should be 90 cm wide.

vii) Stands of polypots on level ground can be bounded by stone, cement block, wooden frame or a wire frame, whichever is most suitable and economic. Whatever the framing the polypot bed should not be sunk below soil level and excess irrigation rain water must be able to drain away easily.

viii) A permanent tree, rock or plastic shade over the nursery does not allow for progressive hardening-off. An artificial shade of wooden post with a wire frame over the top of which are laid maize or sorghum stalks (dried) to provide a 70-80% shade cover is recommended. This shade cover should generally be at a height of at least 1.2 m above the bed surface/top of the polypots.

ix) Properly prepared coffee seed (see Chapter 2) should be sown. Generally speaking the fresher it is the higher will be the germination percentage and the older it is the longer it takes to germinate. Seed known to be of poor quality should not be sown into polypots or nursery beds but into germination beds for transplanting.

x) Spacing of seedlings in germination beds should be 5 x 5 cm, in seedling beds 20 x 20 cm or one seed should be sown in each polypot. A back-up germination bed should be established equal to 20% of the number of pots being sown, to cater for misses. A further allowance of 10 - 20% of the number of polypots sown should be made for 'rogueing' off-type seedlings and runts.

xi) Seed should be sown across the width of the beds rather than along the length of the beds. Planting across the bed can be greatly simplified by using flat planting boards. For germination bed planting these would be 1 m long, 5 cm wide with notches along one edge at 5 cm intervals to make the seed site. For direct sowing in seedling beds the length would be 1.2 - 1.5 m depending upon bed width, 20 cm wide with notches at 15 or 20 cm intervals on both sides of the board to mark the seed sites. Seeds should not be planted closer than 5 cm to the edge of the bed (germination) or 10 cm to the edge of the permanent seedling bed.

xii) Watering must be done with a low pressure supply, through a rose-head sprinkler either from a can with a spout or from a hose (refer (viii) under Small Farmer Nurseries). Never use a high pressure water jet from a hose and never flood irrigate; the former washes soil out of pots or off the beds and the latter causes waterlogging of either a temporary or a permanent nature with loss of soil texture.

xiii) Nitrogen, iron and other nutrient shortages which show up in the leaf colour and patterns (refer to Chapter 10 and Plates 1, 2, 3, 4 and 5) can be controlled with liquid nutrient application via a knapsack sprayer or watering can with a rose-head sprinkler. The inclusion of phosphate fertiliser in the nursery bed or potting compost will insure against shortage of phosphorus. Thus:

Nitrogen - 6 - 8 g/l urea fertiliser at weekly to monthly intervals depending upon leaf colour. Iron, Manganese, Zinc, Boron - monthly application of Fertilon Combi Red spray at the recommended concentration for citrus. Commence sprays at the 2 - 3 true leaf-pair stage.

Phosphorus: into the potting compost, 600 litre volume, add either 500 g single supuphosphate or preferably 225 g double supuphosphate (triple supuphosphate, TSP) mixing in thoroughly.

xiv) Transplant seedlings at the "Helmet" or "Butterfly" stages (refer Plate 6 and Figure 3) never at a later growth stage. Lift and transplant carefully with a pointed planting stick (Figure 3) or a narrow-blade knife.

xv) Harden-off the seedlings progressively from 70 - 80% cover to no shade through three stages at about 6 weekly intervals as described in the Small Farmer Nursery Section (ix). But if the seedling age at transplanting is 9 months, hardening-off will need to begin at 4 months or shortly after this age. Removing shade by day and returning it at night is not a satisfactory method. Shade reduction should be a permanent condition at each stage.

xvi) Strong, vigorous and more drought resistant seedlings which will grow away quickly in the field after transplanting can be grown applying a technique called "undercutting". The technique is more easily applied to polypot seedlings. Holes (2 -3) are made in the base of the pots to encourage the taproot to grow through the bottom of the pot. As soon as this occurs it is cut off at the base of the pot. Thereafter, any further growth below the base of the pot is cut off regularly at 4 - 6 weekly intervals. This treatment stimulates the development of a very prolific and strong lateral root system; simply cutting off the taproot below the polypot when the seedlings are moved for transplanting does not have this beneficial effect, in fact, quite the reverse. Then the action merely removes a large part of the seedling root system leaving behind a much weakened residual root system. This gives slow establishment and high susceptibility to dry/drought conditions.

xvii) Germination beds should be completely covered with fine organic matter after sowing, until the seedlings show above ground. It should then be removed completely or moved into the interrows well clear of the seedlings. Seedlings transplanted into beds should be mulched at the two true leaf stage in the interrows across the bed with either finely broken organic matter (grass, leaves) or with small stones/pebbles. This keeps the soil cool, moist and gives considerably enhanced moisture retention in the surface soil.

xviii) If polypot seedlings are left in the nursery to be carried over to the next planting season, the following actions are necessary to prevent overgrowing and seedling weakness: (a) space the pots wider apart by removing every alternate pot leaving a triangular configuration between rows to allow strong development of lateral branches; (b) cut all the fully open leaves on each seedling in half across the leaf width and discard the distal portion (use as a mulch on top of the pot soil); (c) leave the seedlings unshaded; shading them encourages soft, weak growth.

xix) In existing nurseries where there are sunken polypot beds with permanent cement block surrounds either (a) construct a sloping stone or cement base to drain away excess water or (b) construct a dry stone drain at the base of one side of the bed with drainage outlet, after preparing a compacted sloping soil base for the polypots to stand on.

xx) If bare-root seedlings are being issued by a nursery which have to be carried for a considerable distance in hot, sunny and dry conditions then (a) bundles of seedlings (100/bundle or less as required) should have their roots dipped into either a thick natural clay slurry and then be dried (there are plastic formulations available for this purpose) before transporting and (b) cut off the distal half of all fully open leaves on a seedling. If the leaf cutting is not done and seedlings are wilted at the time of transplanting it should be carried out then to assist with survival and a quick start to growth. Note that the unopened leaf buds on the top of the seedling stem and at the end of any main laterals should not be cut.

xxi) If there is suspicion about the quality of a batch of seed needed for sowing treat as follows: (a) soak in water for 24 hours; (b) germinate as a single layer between two wet jute or sisal (not nylon) sacks. Wet twice a day, morning and evening. Germinate under a full shade cover. Check regularly and plant out very carefully when the white tip of the radicle (root) is just showing. A similar pre-germination of coffee seed can be achieved in a polythene bag of wet vermiculite. Wet the vermiculite (grade size between 2 and 4 mm i.e. passes through a 4 mm sieve but is retained on a 2 mm sieve) thoroughly and squeeze out excess moisture by hand. Mix 3 parts vermiculite with 1 part seed (by volume) and place immediately in the bag. Store in full shade at room temperature, check at 10 - 14 days and re-moisten if necessary; germination should occur after about 3 weeks. Sort out germinated seed carefully and plant out in polypots or seedling bed.

In the seedling bed or polypot nursery careful rogueing of runted or malformed (abnormal) seedlings should be carried out regularly.

Control of pests and diseases in nursery seedlings are discussed and described in Chapter 12.

5. FIELD PLANTING

Problems

The density of coffee tree populations in the ROY is extremely variable and examples are known in different locations which vary from 600 to 700 to 10,000 or more trees/hectare (ha). A general average is probably in the region of 1,500 to 3,000 trees/ha.

The idea of preparing planting holes after lining out and staking tree positions, separating topsoil and subsoil and infilling with topsoil only is not often practised or practised with sufficient care and attention to detail. Frequently a small, shallow hole is scraped out with a single tine hoe, the seedling is forced into it and the surrounding soil returned. An application of organic manure in the planting hole is not always made.

The time of planting out is often erratic and not always related to anticipated rainfall on a proper seasonal basis. The application of irrigation water for a dry season planting is no substitute for natural rainfall conditions for several reasons not the least of which are temperature and atmospheric humidity conditions.

Poor planting of either a poor or a good quality seedling is not the way to start the development of good quality coffee trees. Techniques of temporary seedling shade and shelter, so necessary for seedlings that have not been hardened-off in the nursery and of mulching newly planted seedlings are by no means the general rule.

Spacing

The curve relating the yield of green bean to the number of trees per unit area of land is asymptotic (shaped like a round-topped hill) with a broad apex. In general terms optimal yields under a good basic management standard are obtained with tree populations of between 2,700 to 3,500 tall arabica trees/ha. If these trees are pruned on the multiple stem system with two verticals per tree in the first cycle, and 3 or more in subsequent pruning cycles, best yields with sustained, healthy development are achieved with 5,400 to 7,000 verticals/ha in the first cycle and 10,000 to 12,000 verticals in later cycles. In later cycles the number of verticals/

ha will vary with tree numbers and may be further adjusted to suit a specific environment.

If tall arabica coffee is to be intercropped either in the early years only or for a longer period, the spacing of the tree will need to allow for this. However, in the absence of tree shade and long-term intercropping wide spacing between coffee trees inevitably permits greater weed growth and the need for a greater labour input to control these weeds.

Both square or rectangular and triangular (or staggered) coffee tree arrangements are found in the ROY. Regular spacing of trees is highly desirable to permit standardised pruning, handling and manuring of the trees. Wider spacings tend to be used in lower rainfall areas where irrigation water is not always freely available and where growth is often more rapid and vigorous. Closer spacings are often adopted in cooler areas of climate where growth is slower, rainfall is usually higher and irrigation water is freely available or is less of a necessity for crop production.

Recommended spacings for the regular planting out of coffee trees are:

Spacing (m)	Area per Tree (m^2)	Number of Trees/ha	
		Square Planting	Triangle Planting
2 x 2	4	2,500	__2,880__
2 x 1.5	3	__3,330__	3,830
2.5 x 1.5	3.75	2,660	__3,060__
2.5 x 1.25	3.125	__3,200__	3,696

The underlined population numbers are preferred; the 2 m wide interrow space is for tall coffee that will only be intercropped for the first 2 or at the most 3 years except perhaps when the pruning cycle is changed over (refer Chapter on Pruning). The 2.5 m wide interrow space is for tall coffee that it is intended to intercrop with certain designated crops (refer Chapter (7), Weeding and Intercropping).

Interplanting

Interplanting tall, mature arabica coffee with young coffee seedlings to increase the number of coffee trees/ha should never be done among, or underneath, unpruned trees. If it is done under these conditions (or under tall dense shade tree cover) the new young trees will be weak, growth will be poor and stems will be weak; all these adverse conditions produce low yields of coffee from these trees.

Coffee interplanting, to a regular pattern, either to replace missing trees or to increase the population, should be made when the mature coffee is heavily pruned

Field Planting

back for a change over in the cycle i.e. to produce new, strong, vertical growth (refer Chapter on Pruning).

Holing

Prepare for planting out coffee seedlings in the following way:
i) After clearing and cultivating the land or when planting into an area with an annual legume crop present, mark the planting position clearly with a stick or a large stone.
ii) Before actually planting out (2 - 6 weeks before) excavate the planting hole size 30 cm x 30 cm x 30 cm. Place topsoil (0 - 15 cm) and subsoil (more than 15 cm) separately on either side of the hole. This should be done in the dry season just before the rains arrive or very early after the rains arrive (refer Figure 4).
iii) Loosen the soil at the bottom of the hole to facilitate root development. Large stones should be removed.
iv) Mix with the excavated topsoil 1 - 2 kg of dry organic manure. The mixing should be very thorough (refer Figure 4).

Transplanting

Transplanting may be with polypot or with bare-root seedlings, the latter carefully lifted in the nursery with a fork to avoid root damage. Very great care is necessary to ensure that no seedling is deep-planted i.e. the soil level after planting must not be higher up the stem than it originally was while growing (correctly) in the nursery. The natural division between root and stem must be maintained at or only fractionally below the soil surface. Plate 11 (stone mulching) also illustrates deep planting plus soil movement against the stem; note the '*sahani*' depth which is considerable following soil removal, the 10 - 15 cm of pale coloured stem unearthed and the dark wavy ring around the stem above the pale area, indicating the original height of the soil up the stem. With the bare-root seedlings do not cut off the bottom part of the taproot nor bend it sideways or twist it in any way. The adverse effect on root development due to these planting errors can affect the time between planting out and first yield production, and the yield potential of a tree for many years thereafter. Trees badly planted in this way are more susceptible to the overbearing/dieback syndrome (refer Chapter (11), Physiological Disorders) which is so damaging to both trees and their subsequent yield level.

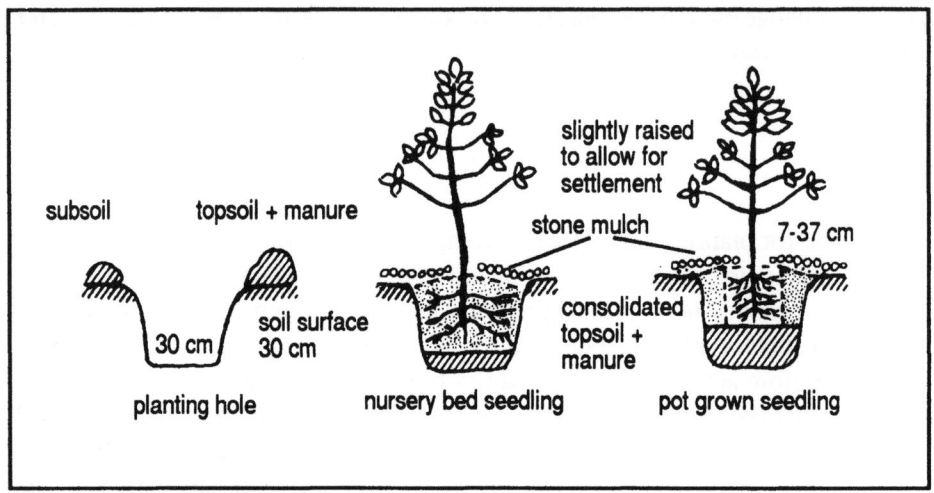

Figure 4: Planting Hole, Nursery and Seedlings Planted Out

i) A bare-root seedling should be held against a side of the hole at the correct depth and the hole filled with the topsoil plus organic manure mixture. If this is insufficient to fill the hole up properly, draw in topsoil from the surrounding soil surface. Do not use the excavated subsoil for infilling but spread it over the surrounding soil surface, specifically wherever topsoil has been taken from.

ii) Bare-root seedlings should not be 'jammed' into a planting hole with the lateral roots hanging downwards. As the topsoil and manure is returned to the hole the lateral roots should be spread out at right angles on top of infill in stages as the hole is filled up. This is a normal procedure for planting tree seedlings and is a very important operation. Good quality polypot seedlings will have the lateral roots growing in this form within the polypot soil mass (refer Figure 4). It is obviously an easier task to plant out polypot than bare-root seedlings, with less chance of poor results.

iii) A polypot seedling will usually have the plastic removed by cutting the side. Place the undisturbed seedling plus soil into the hole at the correct depth to avoid a deep-planting effect. Fill the hole in with topsoil plus organic manure, not subsoil, drawing in more topsoil from the surrounding soil if necessary.

iv) Unless the soil is very wet or rainfall is imminent, the seedlings should be given water after mulching and shading.

v) After planting out the seedlings it will be necessary to shade them from the full sun unless they are fully hardened-off in the nursery (refer Chapter 4. General Nursery Techniques (xi)). This may be achieved with a grass thatch lodged on top of a tripod of three sticks, by small tree branches or a banana leaf overhead or by the use of stones (Plates 9, 10).

vi) The shade should be built inside a basin "*sahani*" around each tree. This may be square or circular with a width or diameter, of about 60 cm across. The surface of the soil inside the *sahani* where water will be applied should be mulched before watering but shortly after planting, with either organic matter (grass, leaf etc.) or small stones (Figure 4, Plates 11, 12). Note that the coffee in Plates 11 and 12 is not newly planted but the photographs illustrate the stone mulching required. It will also be noted that the position of stone mulch in Plate 10 is not the same as recommended here. Where polypot seedlings are sown do not discard the opened plastic pot; fully and carefully opened out it can be used as plastic mulch under part of the stone mulch or held down in the *sahani* by stones. It is important that neither organic material nor stones applied as a soil mulch touch the stem of the seedling (or tree) and a space of 10 cm should be left clear around the seedling (15 cm around the stem of large trees). Shade thinning with organic materials will occur as they rot and decay and as the seedling coffee grows bigger. The seedling coffee will emerge from beneath the stone shade as it grows but after a suitable time the stone cover should be gradually removed preferably in dull and/or wet weather.

vii) The edge or rim of the *sahani* whether circular or square should not be raised by pulling soil away from the seedling (unless it is deep-planted as is apparent with the young tree in Plate 12) but by moving soil inwards from the area outside the *sahani* edge.

viii) At no time should organic manure or soil be heaped up around and against the stem of the coffee seedling (or the stem of any coffee tree). This treatment can have very adverse effects on both growth and yield; it produces the equivalent of a deep-planting effect and can lead to basal stem rots.

ix) The correct time for transplanting coffee seedlings is critical whether irrigation water is available or not. The correct time is early in the main rains when the soil is moist and the atmosphere is humid. As an example take an area where the rains commence in the latter part of March after a hot dry season. The rains should continue until mid-September but June is a dry month. Coffee planting should be planned for either mid-late April or mid-late July preferably the former. A minimum effective rainfall of 100 mm should have fallen before the transplanting operation is done. Suitable timing adjustments will be required for specific local conditions but dry season planting is to be avoided.

6. PRUNING

The Survival of a Healthy Coffee Tree

The single, most significant husbandry operation apart from the necessary use of water with soil mulch for the survival of the coffee tree is the application of a pruning system on a regular annual basis. Pruning is necessary for many reasons some of the more important of which are:

i) to maintain suitable leaf:crop ratio e.g. when there is too much crop for the amount of leaf on a tree the overbearing syndrome develops with consequent tree debility.
ii) to regulate the annual harvest to a crop level that the tree can healthily support under the local environmental conditions.
iii) To attain this cropping level on a regular annual basis.
iv) to open up the trees to light and air so that the desired cropping level is achieved and to reduce or prevent pest and disease attacks.

A well-grown coffee tree responds to regular and careful pruning but where the response is poor it will generally be for one or more of the following reasons:

i) an inherent variety weakness
ii) a malformed root system (poor nursery or transplanting operations)
iii) incorrect timing of the pruning operation and/or poor quality of the pruning operation
iv) poor soil fertility i.e. inability of the tree to respond to the operation
v) unsuitable climatic conditions.

Note that the pruning-off of thin wood (primary, secondary and other branch growth, unwanted suckers) should be done with secateurs and of older, tougher wood (old verticals or major pruning to rejuvenate old trees) the use of a pruning saw is necessary. Hacking away wood with a large slash-knife or an axe generally leaves rough, ragged split wood scars which are particularly damaging on the original or secondary main stem. Such wounds encourage wood rot and termite attack and destroy dormant vertical stem (basal sucker) buds which may be required in later years for tree regeneration.

Problems

Generally there is no adoption and application of a regular annual pruning system in the ROY coffee and this is clearly reflected in many aspects of the field condition of this crop. A loose descriptive name for the present general practice would be "plant and let go" in that there is little planned attempt to adapt the coffee to the conditions.

In this respect it is almost certainly true to state that the generally harsh environment provides the most forcing conditions for arabica coffee in the ROY compared with any other country in which arabica coffee production is a major industry.

The absence of careful pruning is apparent in the field condition of most coffee trees. In particular:

i) In some areas the stated farmer aim is to have 3 or 4 bearing verticals in the early years of the life (say up to 7 years in the field) but in any block of young coffee a range of from 1 to 5 verticals is quite usual.

ii) In the pre-crop early years, young trees are generally well leafed and this leaf has a healthy green colour (Plates 13, 14, 15 and 16).

iii) Following the first 1 to 3 harvests the trees begin to show debility with reduced leaf area, poor leaf colour and poor leafage on older primaries (Plates 17, 18).

iv) Older trees may have 1 or 2 to 11 or more crop verticals (in one example, 17 verticals were counted) some of which are obviously weak i.e. thin and tall, and this proliferation predisposes severe overcropping under most field conditions (Plates 19, 20). This absence of pruning and handling with crop and leaf control leads progressively to early overbearing (see Chapter 11, Physiological Disorders) in on-crop years and the development of extreme biennial or triennial bearing cycles, particularly in unshaded coffee.

v) Improved alternative methods for regeneration/rejuvenation pruning of old 'tired' trees with sound root frames and basal main trunks would be beneficial. This approach is often adopted at times of severe set-back e.g. death by drought of the top growth of a tree, rather than as a general approach with older coffee plantings.

Pruning Methods

The proposed methods for pruning arabica coffee in the ROY are an interpretation of broad systems that can be successful under the observed field conditions.

However, pruning is an area of adaptive research study that requires critical evaluation at the national level to provide proven and precise techniques. The proposals that follow will improve the present situation but will almost certainly be susceptible to refinement for local conditions in some part.

The system proposed may be referred to as a controlled multiple stem system with regular annual handling.

New Young Coffee - 1st Cycle

A. Tall, weak, whippy seedlings

i) With tall, thin, whippy overgrown seedlings with no lateral branch development and little or no leaf left on the stem (Plate 21), cropping verticals (two) need to be encouraged by a special technique. It is known as bending or the Agobiada system and is illustrated diagrammatically in Figure 5 and is shown in Plate 22. Bending should not be done until the seedling is firmly rooted either 10-12 weeks after planting out (at the beginning of the rainy season) or with the onset of the following wet season.

ii) Cut off the tip of the seedling (growing point) to suppress apical dominance and ensure stress from the bend, is greatest over the lower 1/4 to 1/3 of the stem length from where verticals are required. Peg down tip with a forked stick or hold down with a heavy stone (but do not smother the leaves).

iii) When the new suckers (verticals) are 15 cm tall select two only, as nearly 35 - 40 cm height) (about knee high) above the soil level as possible. Cut off the original stem at about 45 - 50 cm above soil level when the new vertical stems are well grown.

B. Strong, well-grown seedlings

i) When these seedlings have developed 4 or 5 pairs of lateral branches (Plate 23) either about 12 weeks after planting out if this was done in the first period referred to in Chapter 5, Transplanting (ix) or just prior (3 - 6 weeks) to the onset of the following rainy season, the main stem should be capped 3 - 5 cm above the 4th or 5th lateral pair (Figure 5, second part) at a height of 45 cm above ground level. This produces a skirt of primaries and 2 vertical heads for cropping.

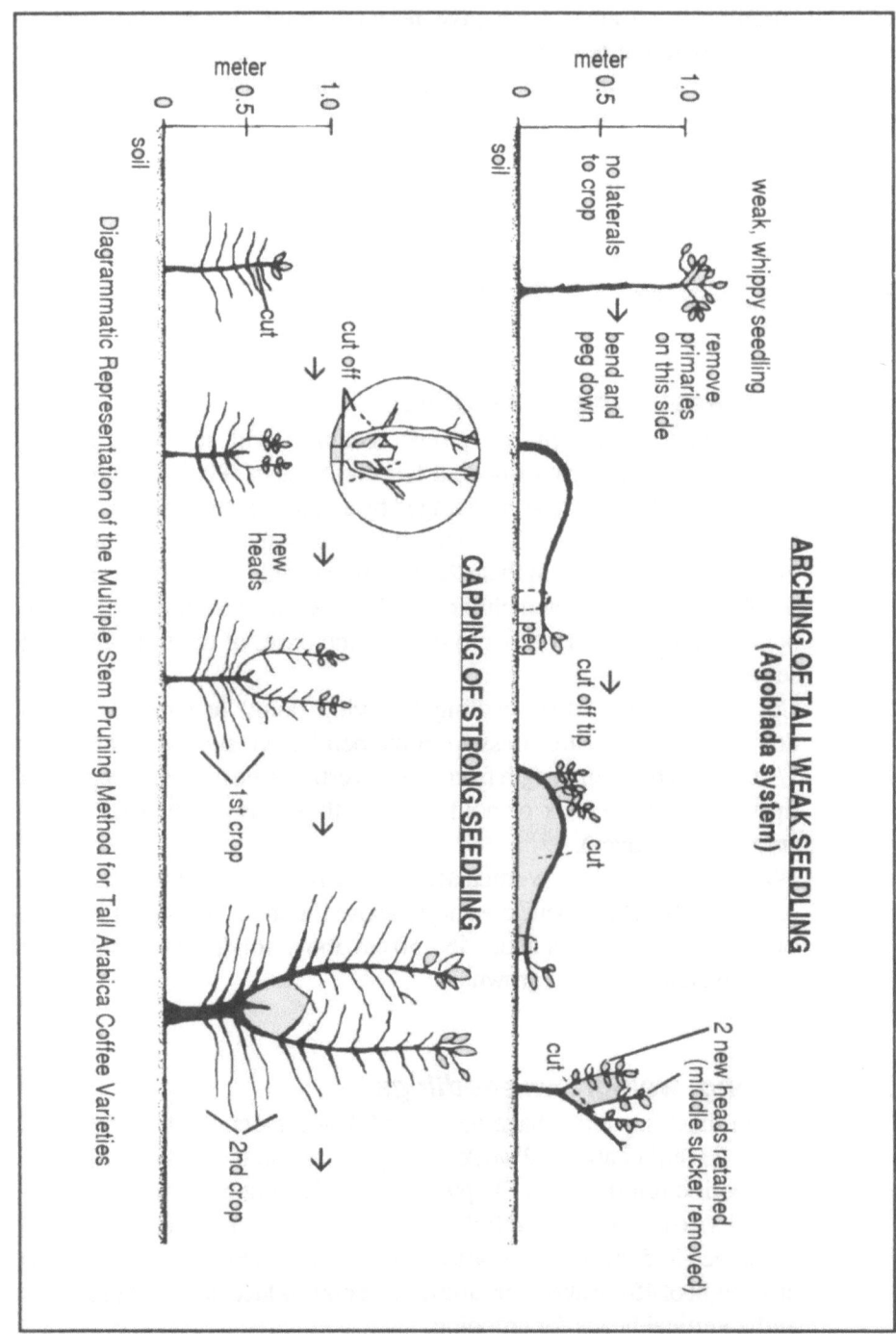

Figure 5: Early Pruning of Young Coffee Trees

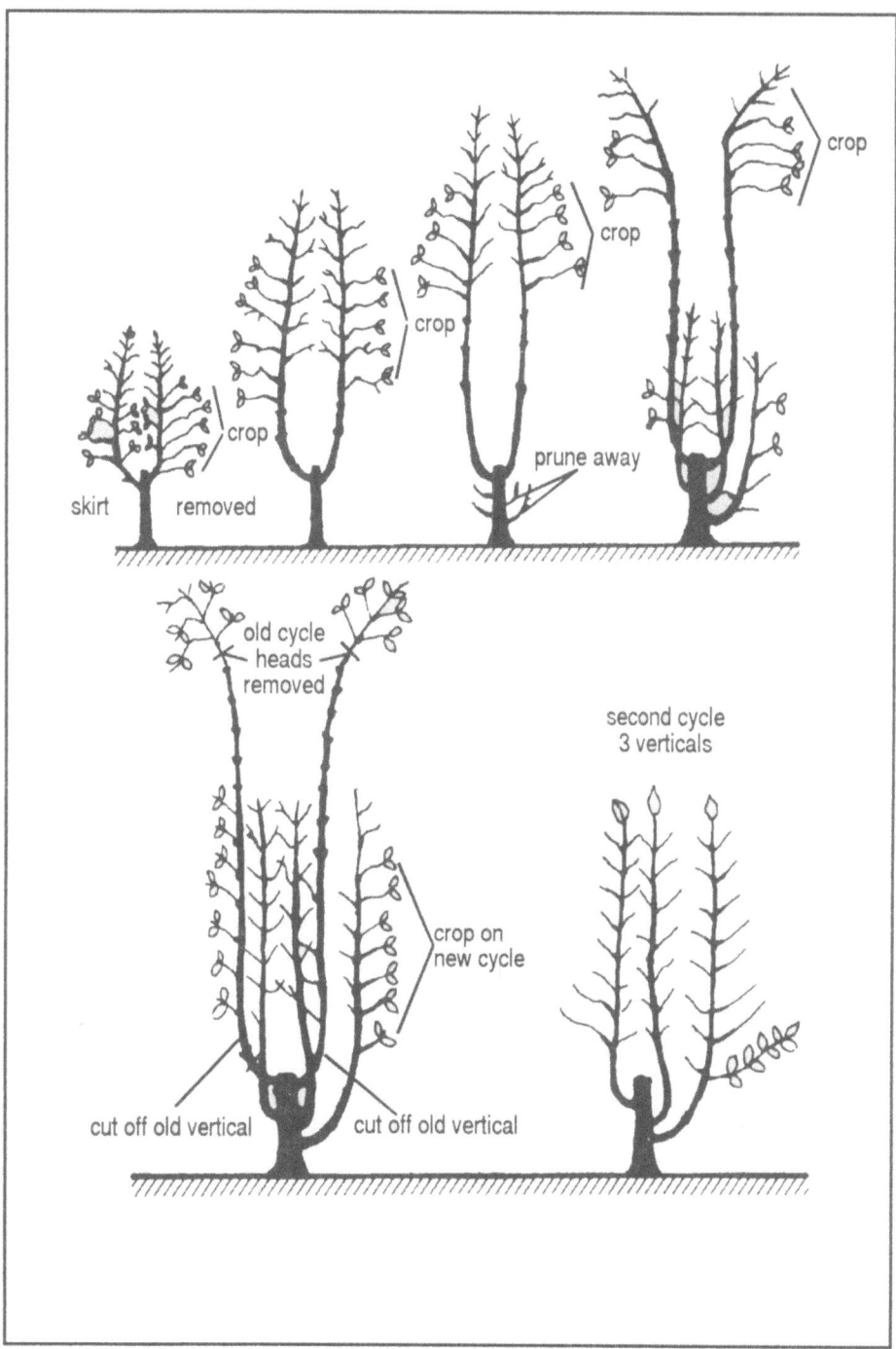

Figure 5 (contd.): Early pruning of Young Coffee Trees

ii) When the two verticals have grown up to 10 - 15 cm tall the uppermost pair of lateral branches are carefully removed (see circled diagram in Figure 5). This is to prevent them creating a notch in the base of the developing verticals which later in life when they have grown tall and are heavy with crop, will be a weak point where the verticals may break off.

iii) Main annual pruning is now simple. Each lateral is allowed to crop for two seasons only and is then cut off. The diagram in Figure 5 illustrates progression until the new second cycle of 3 verticals is achieved.

iv) Where shade trees are present it is probably better to leave only one old cropping head at the end of the cycle when conversion is being made; two are shown in Figure 5. This helps to avoid overshading and lack of light reaching the base of the coffee tree.

v) The actual duration of a cycle will vary with environmental conditions, longer at high cool sites than at low warm sites where growth is faster and cropping is more precocious (forced).

vi) The limitation to two verticals only in the first cycle is obtained by capping which slows down development of the tree and imposes restraint on cropping levels in environmentally forcing conditions. This is deliberate to reduce early cropping levels and so allow a good strong, extensive development of the permanent root system. Heavy cropping in the early years will reduce root development and may result in dieback of the root system particularly if there is overbearing and general tree debility.

vii) At the end of each harvest period, as soon as possible after the last vestiges of crop are removed, carry out the main pruning. This involves (a) cutting off all primary branches that have carried two crops; (b) clearing out the "funnel" i.e. a clear space around each vertical and the tree centre, by removing all secondary growth on the remaining primaries that originate within 15 - 20 cm away from the vertical stem(s).

viii) In this and the one or two subsequent seasonal handlings all sucker growth must be removed together with any secondary or tertiary branches growing upwards or downwards in the vertical plane.

ix) Never retain a vertical or cropping head that originates on the main stem at or below soil level. This situation is frequently noted, particularly where soil has been heaped around the main stem of the tree.

2nd and Subsequent Cycles

In the second and subsequent pruning cycles the number of verticals per tree will be increased to bring the total/ha up to 10 - 12,000 (see Chapter 5, Spacing). Conversion to a new cycle is started when yield levels from the two cropping heads of the first cycle decline; this is principally attributable to the short length of weaker primary growth at the top of old vertical stems.

   i) In Figure 5 six crops from the first cycle are shown though this may vary from 5 to 7 crops (on average) depending upon growing conditions. It will be noted that for the last crop on the two old verticals illustrated in Figure 5 the inside primaries have been cut off. This is to allow maximum light to reach the base of the tree and to facilitate bending outwards of these verticals to allow more room for the new cycle of verticals to develop. It will also be noted that the new cycle (2nd cycle) is shown with 3 verticals in Figure 5 but this may be increased to 4 or 5 verticals depending upon tree population density and local tree vigour.
   ii) At the end of the harvest from the old verticals when it is apparent that the new verticals will crop in the following season, these old verticals are carefully cut off flush with the main stem using a saw. Major pruning of this type should never be done with a large knife or an axe which will only leave split and ragged wounds on the stem.
   iii) Successful conversion to the second and later pruning cycles depends upon the production of good, strong suckers followed by careful selection; retention of well spaced suckers selected when they are 20 - 30 cm tall, arising at the correct height on the main coffee stump frame is essential. The main frame stem was cut at a height of 45 cm above ground level; verticals for the new cycle should be selected at a height of from 15 to 30 cm above ground level though in practice 15 to 40 or 45 cm is quite normal.
   iv) The new verticals of the second cycle are then pruned in the manner illustrated in Figure 5 for the first cycle.
   v) Cycle length may vary with the presence or absence of overhead tree shade being, in general terms, shorter in high altitude, cooler conditions and longer in low altitude, warmer conditions when shade is present. The multiple stem system is flexible and easily modified for a range of conditions.

Thus, if the tendency in a particular area is for the coffee to overbear, cutting up at the time of annual pruning can be extended upwards beyond the primaries that have carried two seasons' crops to some primaries that have only cropped once. This leaves a shorter cropping head to avoid overbearing and/or aid recovery of the tree from a very heavy previous seasons' crop.

One of the objectives of a grower should be to have all the trees in a single block in one standard condition i.e. each tree with the same number of verticals, each with the same length of head on each vertical. Pruning uniform block coffee is then very straightforward as opposed to having to treat each tree on its individual merit.

However, parts of a coffee block or several different coffee blocks may be pruned in the standard manner but be at different stages in the cycle. This is to avoid having all the coffee in a low-cropping conversion stage of a cycle at one time.

Rejuvenation/Regeneration of Old Coffee

Old coffee trees that have gone into yield decline (Plate 20) or mature, unpruned coffee trees (Plate 25) may be rejuvenated/regenerated, provided the mainstem is healthy and free of serious rot or termite damage; such trees must also have an apparently healthy, well developed root system. This may be determined by grasping the stem and assessing anchorage in the ground when trying to rock the tree backwards and forwards.

Both old single stem and multiple stem trees can be converted by one or several methods. The basic approach is either clean stumping or half pruning and these systems are illustrated in Figures 6 and 7.

To generate a new strong growth of basal suckers from which to select the required number of new verticals for future cropping, a basic essential is light at the bottom of the coffee stump frame. In unshaded coffee this requires the removal of at least half of the tree in such a way as to maximise light penetration (refer Figure 6).

In shaded coffee the first pre-requisite is to 'lift' the shade tree cover up by cutting off all branches below 3 - 5 m above the height of the old coffee trees, to leave at least 3 m above the old trees clear of shade tree branches.

The pruning should be done 3 - 6 weeks before the onset of the main wet season is expected.

In most climates where rainfall quantity and timing is reliable clean stumping can be very successful; in marginal or unreliable rainfall areas death of stumped trees may be high.

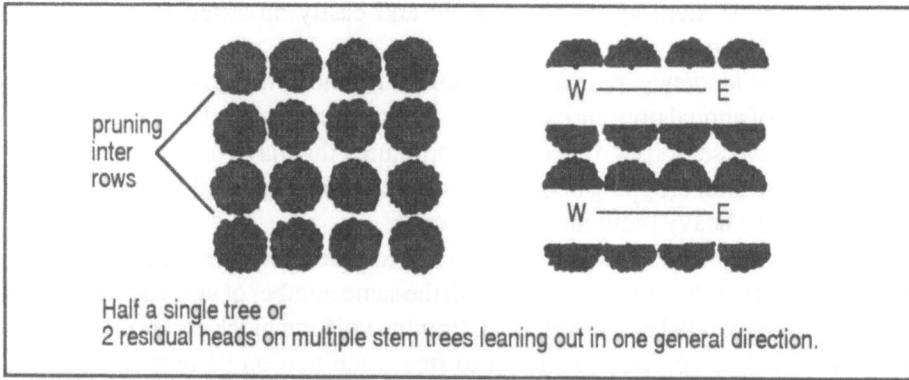

Figure 6: Pruning Single and Multiple Stem

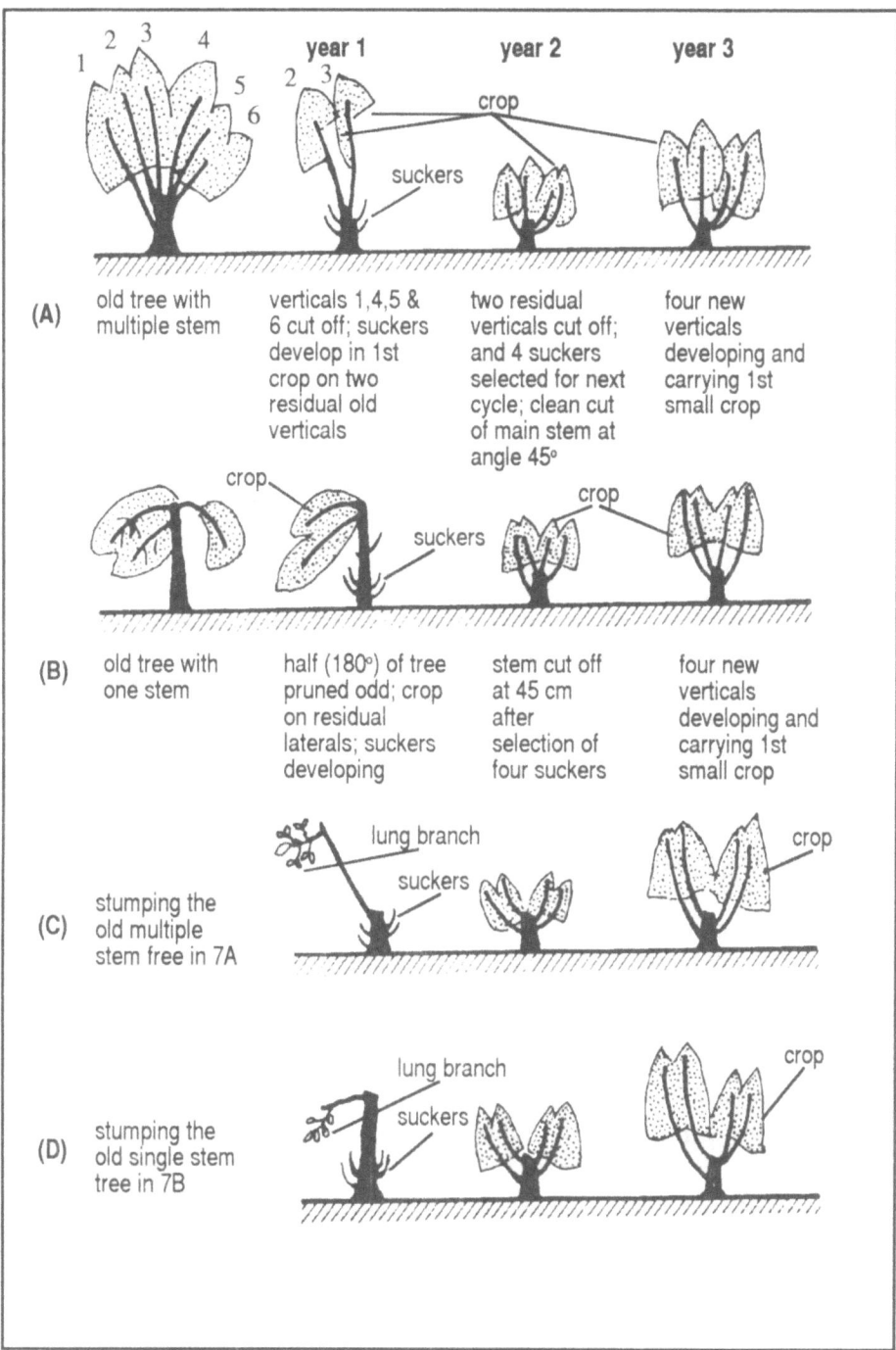

Figure 7: Rejuvenation/Regeneration of Old Coffee Trees

Clean stumping also means no crop at all for at least one season and maybe for two seasons where new growth is slow. Stumping at the wrong time in the coffee season can also extend the period of zero crop production.

If in doubt it is always advisable when clean-stumping to leave a 'lung' or 'mama' branch on the stump to keep it alive in the early stages (refer Figure 7).

Rejuvenation/regeneration conversion of old trees may be done in one of the following ways:

i) Old, single or multiple stem coffee. Select single sound main stem and cut back to 45 cm above ground level. Cut cleanly with a saw at an angle of 45°. Prune off all other growth but retain a 'lung' or 'mama' branch until the new suckers develop (refer Figure 7 C and D).

ii) With single stem trees, converting them to either a new single or as recommended for the ROY, to a new multiple stem cycle, prune off half of the circumference 6 weeks or less before the onset of the main rains (refer Figures 6 and 7B).

iii) With old multiple stem trees, cut off all except two old vertical heads (refer Figure 7A) most suitable for further cropping. Then remove old primary branches by cutting up to leave a small head for crop (approx. 1 m long) and to let light into the base of the tree (Figure 7A).

iv) Take one or two small crops off the half single stem tree or from the two old multiple stem tree heads while the suckers for the new verticals are developing but cut all the old wood off as it becomes apparent that the new developing head(s) will set their first crop.

v) Never overlap the cropping on the old and new tree verticals as this will greatly weaken development of the latter.

vi) In all these methods the key to a successful rejuvenation is the production of strong suckers on the retained coffee tree main frame which is 45 cm tall, followed by careful selection of strong well spaced suckers for the new verticals, when they are 20 - 30 cm tall. The position of these selected suckers should be above 15 cm from ground level, say 15 - 30 cm above ground level, though in practice 15 - 40 or 45 cm is quite usual.

vii) In areas where goats and sheep are grazed in coffee regularly they need to be kept out altogether when coffee is converted to a new cycle to avoid damage to the suckers. Alternatively, in some coffee growing areas outside the ROY, new pruning cycles are developed on tall main frame stems at a height of 1 - 2 m above soil level where the animals cannot reach them. This system necessitates harvesting the crop with a ladder or stable tripod frame.

viii) Where the coffee tree plantation is very dense, growth is weak and trees are old requiring rejuvenation, it is important to thin the population to not less than 1.25 - 1.5 m between trees before starting the pruning.

ix) Note that timing is significant for rejuvenation work. If clean stumping with a 'lung' or 'mama' branch is adopted, the time to commence work is about 6 weeks before the main rains are expected. If conversion is to be by chasing old crop verticals off with the new replacement verticals, the pruning of the residual old verticals and the cutting off of the remainder should be done as soon after harvesting is completed as possible.

x) The 'lung' or 'mama' branch is removed and the stump frame reduced to its final shape as soon as the suckers are well established. References to coffee pruning abound and examples are noted in the literature list (1, 2, 3, 11, 12).

7. WEEDING AND INTERCROPPING

Weed control

Weed control in coffee is an essential requirement for good cropping and growing other commercial or food crops with coffee influences this problem in several different ways.

In this text intercropping of coffee refers to a regular pattern of coffee (in lines) with the other crops grown in the interrow space. Mixed cropping denotes a more random arrangement of coffee with other crops which may often be fruit trees of different kinds.

While it is desirable during the wet season or after irrigating coffee to control and remove soft weeds i.e. broad leaved weeds, it is essential to control and eliminate perennial grass weeds at all times. The commonest of these are *Cynodon* sp. and the sedge grass known as nutgrass (*Cyperus* sp.)

Land for new coffee plantings must be free of grass weeds, particularly perennial grass species. At all times the *sahani* under and around the tree must be free of all weeds. The *sahani* will be 60 cm square or if circular in shape with a 60 cm diameter and it should be covered with mulch, organic if possible but otherwise of stones.

Control of weeds will generally be a manual operation in keeping with the 'organic coffee production' concept. There are many agricultural chemicals available for weed control in coffee provided that water is freely available for spray mixes. Three that are generally used are:

a) Glyphosate. 36% ml (miscible liquid). 2.8 - 5.6 l/ha in 250 l/ha or 204 ml/20 l spray. This chemical kills all plant growth and coffee is no exception, by contact but is not taken up from the soil. It is suitable for grass and 'soft' weeds but repeat application may be necessary to eradicate dense nut grass (*Cyperus* sp.) infestation.

b) Fusilade W (25% a.i.). 4 - 6 l in 250 l/ha or 320 - 480 ml/20 l spray. This chemical is grass specific on contact and will not harm coffee.

c) Paraquat (Grammoxone) 20% ml. 1 l in 250 l/ha or 160 ml/20 l spray. This chemical is a contact weedkiller for all vegetation and will damage coffee if it is accidentally sprayed onto the leaves. It is not taken up from the soil by plants.

If chemical weed control is practised in coffee, care is needed with the equipment used. A manually operated knapsack sprayer and a coarse droplet size jet at low pressure is recommended to avoid spray drift causing damage to the coffee foliage. One such unit is the Cooper-Pegler CP15 (15 l tank capacity) or CP3 (20 l tank capacity) at the 1 kg/cm2 pressure setting with a single 'red' polijet nozzle.

Intercropping

Where coffee is planted in lines the interrow spaces are kept free of weeds most economically by growing rainfed crops during the first two seasons of the new coffee planting. Intercrops should not be planted closer to a young coffee tree than 60 cm to avoid serious competition for soil moisture and plant nutrients.

Reference to coffee spacing in Chapter 5 allows for short-term or long-term interplanting; no special coffee spacing is advised for mixed cropping. Annual intercrops may be maize, sorghum, millet, legumes/pulses or vegetables. The dried stalks (stover) of maize or sorghum may be left in the ground to provide a temporary shelter, windbreak and shade in the dry season following coffee planting.

Mixed cropping may include tall, short- or long-term tree crops like banana, papaya or citrus together with annual crop planting. While spacing of the tree crops will vary with their eventual size and spread, 3 to 6 cm for papaya or banana and 10-20 cm for citrus and larger trees is quite usual.

There is insufficient information and data about coffee intercropping and mixed cropping in the ROY on which to base precise recommendations at this time. However, it should be noted that bananas are very competitive with coffee for soil water, nitrogen and potassium nutrients and require to be well manured and irrigated in the season to prevent deleterious competition with the coffee tree. Furthermore, banana stools in coffee should be restricted very rigidly to a bearing stem, a follower and one peeper (sucker). Uncontrolled banana stools can become overly large to the severe detriment of the coffee.

Where semi-perennial or perennial crops are planted with irrigated coffee, care is necessary to ensure that their position fits into the irrigation water application system for the coffee and the other crops. This may involve replacing a coffee tree with another tree crop where the coffee is spaced regularly rather than planting in the coffee interrow.

8. SHADE AND SHELTER

In its natural environment arabica coffee grows underneath a forest tree shade cover; when grown without shade, higher temperature and light intensity (incoming radiant energy) produce conditions for a potentially higher level of cropping with a greatly increased chance of overbearing through the inability of the tree to meet the needs for nutrients. Alternatively the supplies of nutrients and moisture from the soil may be wholly or seasonally inadequate to meet heavy crop production needs.

Since overbearing is a major physiological condition in much of the ROY coffee with the consequent problems this creates for future crops (refer Chapter 11) it is true to state that in general the coffee would benefit from a degree of shade.

On the other hand in areas where strong and/or persistent winds occur regularly at certain times of the day or night and particularly when dry desiccating winds occur in the dry season, shelter for the coffee will be beneficial.

Shade is provided in several forms notably:

i) Topographical shade in mountainous areas where some slopes are in shade for a part of the day.

ii) In all areas some cloud cover occurs to obscure the sun if only in the wet season. If such conditions also occur in the dry season as they do in some areas, this factor will be significant. The occurrence of either (a) and/or (b) conditions will modify any further actions to introduce a shade cover into coffee plantings.

iii) Self shade or mutual shade provided within a coffee tree and between adjacent coffee trees. Planting density, the configuration e.g. triangular versus square or rectangular geometry and pruning method are concerned with this situation.

iv) Shade tree planting within the coffee stand; the trees may be either a non-commercial or commercial species, the latter of one type or mixed species.

v) Temporary shade provided in coffee for the establishment period, say the first 2 or 3 seasons, by small tree or shrubs or by leaving tall standing crop residues in the coffee e.g. maize or sorghum stalks left over from intercropping.

Shelter from adverse winds can be provided by topography, mutual shelter by the coffee trees themselves, by permanent or temporary shade trees and by crop residues.

Some of the effects of overhead tree shade are to reduce:
- i) sunlight intensity
- ii) air temperature by day and it protects coffee from low night temperatures at high altitudes or in valley bottoms into which cold air may distil at night.
- iii) soil temperature
- iv) evaporation of moisture from the soil surface
- v) soil erosion by breaking the force of the rain i.e. impact upon the soil surface and by increasing drainage
- vi) the transpiration rate of the coffee.

It also:
- vii) protects the coffee from wind and hail damage
- viii) prevents the physiological disorder of 'hot and cold' and 'crinkle leaf' (refer Chapter 11)
- ix) provides plant nutrients brought up from the deeper parts of the soil profile and returned to the topsoil in the leaf fall.
- x) depresses weed growth in coffee particularly perennial and other grasses.

Shade tree planting in coffee has some major disadvantages which need careful consideration:
- i) in the harsh climates of the ROY with a 5-6 month dry season and relatively low rainfall, competition with the coffee for available soil moisture may outweigh the overall benefit of the shade effect. Under these conditions an adequate and reliable source of water for irrigation is essential if shade trees are to be planted. This would not be significant in wadis where surface and/or sub-surface ground water is present all year round.
- ii) shade trees require careful regulation to maintain the proper height of the shade above the coffee trees and the requisite density of the cover.
- iii) when shade trees die, are removed, thinned, pruned or broken by the wind or by lightning, there may be some damage to the coffee beneath.

The overriding consideration with respect to shade tree planting in coffee is that there must be adequate soil moisture, natural or supplemented by irrigation, to avoid any competition for soil moisture between the coffee and the shade tree.

The ideal permanent shade tree would be:
- i) as long-lived as the coffee
- ii) the wood must not be brittle
- iii) growth must be fairly rapid

iv) it must respond to training to produce a clear straight trunk for at least 4 or 5 to 7 m above ground level
v) it should then branch out with a spreading habit i.e. an umbrella shape
vi) leaves should be feathery
vii) the tree must not be leafless during the hottest time of the year
viii) the root system should be deep and not surface-spreading (plate-like) to minimise competition with the coffee.
ix) it should not have any adverse effect on adjacent coffee nor should it be a host of coffee pests and diseases.

While no tree has yet been found with all these qualities they do serve as a basis for shade tree assessment and allow emphasis to be placed on priority characters for a particular situation. Of course, if natural forest tree cover is thinned to provide coffee shade it is difficult to select for all the most desirable characters among those listed here.

In the ROY consideration of permanent shade tree planting, desirable though it may be could be broadly categorised as follows:-

a) Coffee at higher altitudes + adequate irrigation water supply - tree shade
b) Coffee at higher altitudes + good rainfall + some irrigation water supply - tree shade
c) Coffee at higher altitudes + low or erratic rainfall + variable irrigation water supply - no shade
d) Coffee at higher altitudes + good rainfall and no irrigation water - no shade
e) Coffee at lower altitudes + good rainfall + irrigation water supply - tree shade
f) Coffee at lower altitudes + good rainfall + unreliable irrigation water in dry season - no shade
g) Coffee at lower altitudes + low erratic rain + erratic irrigation water supply in dry season - no shade

Basically an adequate and reliable dry season irrigation water supply is a requirement for shade trees to be planted into coffee plots at any altitude in the ROY because of the rainfall distribution pattern with the long hot dry season.

Closer spacing for coffee plantings and the triangular field configuration such that self shade and shelter is maximised are given in Chapter 5.

Where the shade that is interplanted into regularly spaced coffee is commercial the spacing will tend to favour the commercial species and planting will be made in the interrow spaces between coffee lines. In square or rectangular coffee spacings planting should be on the diagonal intersection between four coffee trees. Where the distance between coffee tree rows is 2 - 2.5 m, the spacing for tall banana stools for example, will be of the order of about 7 x 7 m (225/ha) as a staggered planting

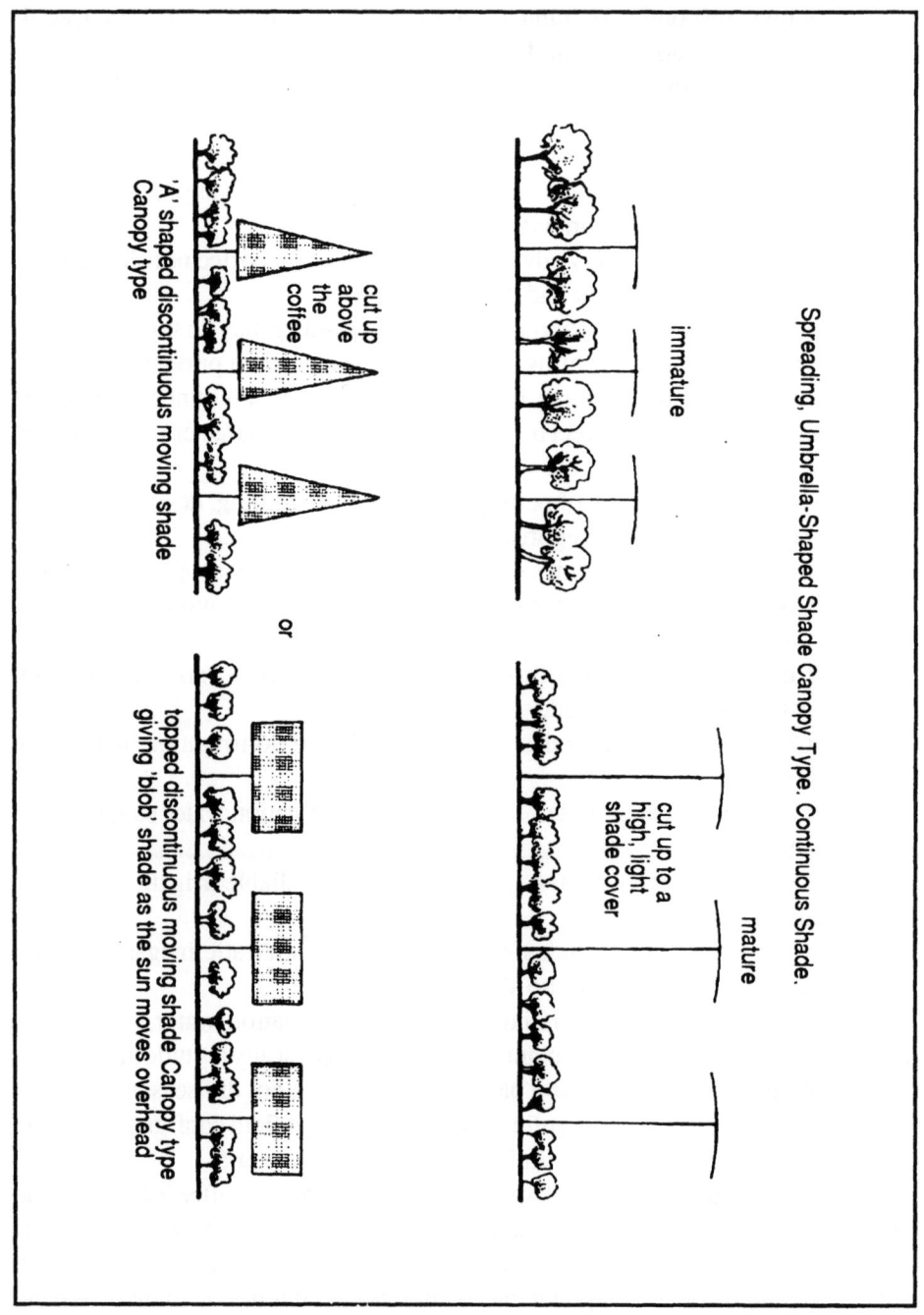

Figure 8: Possible Shapes of Shade Trees

along the interrow. A similar spacing would apply to tall papaya fruit plants but citrus, depending upon tree size, would need to be 10 x 10 m (100/ha) or more apart.

When a non-commercial shade tree species is planted into regularly spaced coffee it is best to plant in the coffee tree line substituting the shade tree for a coffee tree. For the first 2 - 3 seasons while the permanent trees grow up (they should be planted at the same time as the coffee trees) temporary shade/shelter may be beneficial e.g. maize or sorghum stalks left standing, Optimum shade tree spacing will vary with tree size and shape but as an example the *Cordia* sp. that is seen in the coffee should be planted at about 20 x 20 m square.

The pruning and handling of non-commercial shade trees has the objective of providing a high and light shade cover. The extent of the shade density should be that obtained with 30-35% of shade effect over the coffee as soon as the trees have grown up. Furthermore, as the shade trees develop in young coffee, the lowest branches should not be less than 1 - 2 m above the tops of the coffee trees; in mature coffee this height should be 3 - 5 m above the tops of the coffee trees, depending upon the shade tree species. However, a general rule is that the denser the shade cover the higher it should be above the coffee tree. In Plate 24 the 30 year old coffee is much too heavily shaded by unpruned shade trees that are not high enough above the tops of the coffee trees.

Figure 8 shows diagrams of immature and mature canopy or 'umbrella' shaped tree shade and shade trees with an 'A' rather than a canopy shape which may be topped to provide 'blob' shaped shade. While all shade cover is moving as the sun traverses during the day, a fine 'stippled' shade is provided by a fine-leaved umbrella canopy but moving 'blobs' of shade are provided by the 'A' shaped trees which may be improved by topping to encourage lateral growth.

The value of shade and the management of both non-commercial and commercial shade tree species is a subject requiring practical study in the ROY.

9. IRRIGATION, WATER USE AND MULCHING

Once good quality seedlings have been produced in the nursery and carefully planted out in the field to be managed under a planned pruning system which optimises tree health and quality coffee production, efficient water use associated with conservation mulching becomes the next most important factor.

It seems certain that while the quantity and quality of water available for coffee irrigation will fluctuate with rainfall totals and distribution, and the ground water reserves with longer term climatic conditions, greater demands with time and future developments will mean a generally scarcer natural resource. Greater water use efficiency in coffee plantings is therefore a major factor for consideration, to be coupled with maximum conservation of both natural and irrigation water in the soil. Such an approach should be less expensive with both labour and water.

Conservation of natural (rainfall) or irrigation water in the soil can be achieved by mulching the soil surface. This has the added advantage of encouraging the development of feeder root bearers and feeder roots in the top 15 cm of the soil which is the richest level of the profile in both minerals and organic matter. Generally, coffee mulching is down with organic matter (crop residues, dead weeds, fallen leaves, waste coffee skins, compost and coarse cattle manure). In the ROY organic matter is fed to animals and coffee skins are used for preparing 'Gishr'; neither are generally available for mulching. However, it is generally effective to mulch with stones to substantially reduce evaporative soil moisture losses. This is not a general practice in the ROY although it is adopted in limited areas (Plates 10, 17 and 25).

Irrigation

Irrigation water may be applied to coffee:
i) as a supplement to rainfall failure or deficiency in the usually wet season
ii) In the dry season to extend the natural wet season at both the end and the beginning, so reducing the 5 - 6 month dry season to a more tolerable 2-3 months for the coffee
iii) Emergency application to save coffee trees in unforeseen situations.

It is said that on average coffee is irrigated 12 - 16 times a year; for a 5 month dry season or a 5 month dry season and a dry June this is an average of 2 to 3 irrigations per month. Effective mulching could reduce the number of irrigation operations by 25 to 33 per cent.

To obtain the greatest benefit from the least volume and frequency of water application it is important to time irrigation treatments very carefully. The timing should be related to the available soil moisture and the physiological condition of the coffee tree i.e. growth, flowering and cropping rhythms as dictated by natural climatic conditions; thus irrigation is an essential climatic support system in the ROY but it should not dictate the physiological rhythms of the coffee tree which it will do if it is misused. Since there is effectively one wet and one dry season, the latter of 5 - 6 months duration, coffee irrigation should be phased in this manner:

i) to extend the end of the natural rains season into the dry season by at least 6 - 8 weeks i.e. maintain moist soil conditions with minimal moisture stress within the coffee tree. Do not allow the top 50 - 75 cm of soil to dry down to more than 1/3rd of the available water holding capacity. The presence of a mulch cover on the soil surface is essential (organic or stone) and from the end of this irrigation period the soil under the mulch will slowly dry out over a period of 4 - 8 weeks.

ii) To advance the beginning of the wet season and so reduce the dry season period to about 2 months. At this point in time, 6 - 8 weeks before the main rainy season can be expected to arrive, commence irrigating again. This anticipates the arrival of the rains and should trigger off the major blossoming. Moist soil conditions must then be maintained under the mulch cover until the rains arrive.

iii) Since June is often a dry month due to a pause in the rainfall season, irrigation water application may be necessary to support crop development and to prevent serious water stress in the tree with associated berry and leaf fall. Coffee that is stone-mulched will be less susceptible than unmulched coffee because stressful dry soil conditions will develop more slowly and may often be much less severe.

Water Use

For reasons of economy in regularly spaced coffee it is more economical to apply water to each tree in a *'sahani'* that extends to the drip circle: the shape of the *sahani* may be square or circular. Irrigating an area extending from the coffee stem outwards to the edge of the drip circle will ensure that water reaches a majority of the feeder root system. Concentrating irrigation water in the soil where most of the coffee roots are is both effective and economical. The boundary or bund forming the individual free *sahani* should be made by pulling soil inwards from the interrow area and not by pulling soil outwards away from the coffee stems, thereby exposing fine roots or at least driving them deeper into the soil in future development. This is more economical than surface irrigating a whole terrace or the entire soil surface of a large bunded basin containing several trees e.g. a broad based terrace cross bunded to contain water over the whole soil surface for several coffee trees. To apply measured quantities of water to individual trees does require delivery through a flexible pipe at low pressure although on newly planted seedlings it may be measured in and applied from a bucket or other plastic/metal container.

The following table shows the approximate volumes of water that need to be applied to individual tree *sahanis* of varying shape and size to provide the water equivalent of either 50 or 100 mm rainfall to that bunded soil area.

Size of *Sahani* (cm)		Volume of Irrigation (litre/*sahani*)	
Square	Circular	Square	Circular
		(for 50 mm or 200 mm rainfall)	
40 x 40	46 (diameter)	8	16
60 x 60	68 (")	18	36
80 x 80	92 (")	32	64
100 x 100	112 (")	50	100

Measuring the approximate quantity of water applied from a pipe at a steady water pressure can be determined quite simply by measuring the time taken to deliver a known volume in litres e.g. by timing the filling of a bucket or basin of known volume. The delivery time per *sahani* then adjusted for the required volume depending upon the size of the *sahani*.

Mulching with Stones

Accepting that with the possible exception of newly planted coffee seedlings in the field, organic materials are not generally available for use as a mulch in coffee, then stone mulching is the logical alternative. In many parts of the ROY where coffee is grown, stones are in abundant supply for this purpose. While the size of the stones used is not important, smaller stones will be easier to apply underneath young, small trees; what is important is that they should fit together as completely as possible, side by side, to provide as complete a cover as possible above the soil surface. Note that:

i) The tree *sahani* base should be flat and level within the bund (raised edge) before the stone mulch is applied. In Plates 11 and 12 it will be noted that the *sahani* bottom is flat but lies below the surrounding soil level. This arose because silt and soil had been moved into the area around the trees by past irrigation and it was necessary to correct the "deep planting" effect (refer Chapter 5).

ii) The recommended position for a stone mulch is underneath the trees in the irrigation '*sahani*'. Other positions are used; in Plate 10, the ground is stone mulched except underneath or around the tree and in young coffee this method provides no real soil protection above the roots of the young trees. The stones near the tree in Plate 10 are part of a stone shade that was removed to allow for irrigation. In Plate 25, for older coffee the entire soil surface is completely stone mulched which is very good but would make wet season intercropping difficult if it were to be practised. When coffee trees are planted close together in the row e.g. at a spacing of 2 x 1.5 m or 2.5 x 1.25 m (refer Chapter 5), the stone mulch would be best as a continuous line along the row when the trees have grown older i.e. are three or more years in the field.

iii) When a stone mulch is applied around a coffee tree in a *sahani* the stones should not rest against the coffee stem; there should be a space of 10 cm wide that is clear of stones. This is to prevent the coffee stem from remaining wet for long periods after rainfall or irrigation for if this happens there is a risk of fungal infection of the stem.

iv) Where the recommended multiple stem pruning system is adopted (see Chapter 6) it is obvious that with cutting up of the branches, the soil beneath unshaded coffee trees will be directly exposed to more sunlight. A similar situation will occur with a cycle conversion and when older coffee is subjected to regeneration/rejuvenation pruning. It is essential that there is a stone mulch over the soil underneath the trees to reduce evaporation and organic matter loss from the topsoil. Thus pruning and stone mulching should be an husbandry partnership.

v) Reference was made earlier in this Chapter to the value of a good mulch cover of the soil in reducing the number of irrigation rounds in a season. Prevention of evaporation of soil moisture derived from both rainfall and irrigation could reduce the number of irrigations by 25 per cent or more. This will be particularly noticeable where the depth of soil is 0.75 - 1 m or greater and when the soil itself contains much gravel or coarse stone as these greatly reduce the retention of plant available water within the soil profile.

vi) When organic manure is applied to stone mulched coffee trees the mulch cover should be temporarily removed from the *sahani* and replaced as soon after the manure has been applied and lightly worked into the topsoil with minimal damage to the fine coffee root system. In general, the same procedure would apply if inorganic fertiliser were being applied to the coffee.

It is concluded that the use of stone mulches in the ROY arabica coffee is one practice by which the husbandry can be improved with benefit. The benefits may be summarised as:

i) when associated with the use of organic manure underneath the stone mulch the topsoil structure will be improved.
ii) There will be improved rainfall acceptance and infiltration into the soil.
iii) There will be conservation of topsoil moisture through reduced evaporative loss and greater soil water holding capacity.
iv) It can control any tendency for soil movement.
v) It shades the soil and reduces soil temperature thereby conserving organic matter. It maintains a more even soil temperature.
vi) It stimulates feeder root production in the richer topsoil.
vii) It interacts beneficially for irrigated coffee by reducing the seasonal water needs of the crop and so means less frequent irrigation rounds.

10. MANURE AND FERTILISER

Neither fertiliser nor micronutrient applications will provide a universal panacea for coffee in the ROY. The exception is only where nutrient is so limiting that it severely constrains growth, production and quality. Economic use is dependent upon good basic husbandry being practised, a factor which severely reduces their value on much of the ROY coffee today. Thus, in general terms the application of fertiliser to the ROY coffee would not be generally recommended until husbandry standards are improved.

Furthermore, the use of dry animal manure which is currently the source of plant nutrients and soil organic matter, needs to be associated with improved husbandry and application for the best results e.g. burying it in pits at one point of the compass or heaping it up close around the coffee stem are not 'best-use' techniques.

The most serious mineral deficiencies usually observed are nitrogen (N) which has a very significant influence on overbearing and iron (Fe) due to high soil pH levels which very adversely affect bean quality i.e. raw, roast and liquor. In large nurseries some symptoms of zinc (Zn), Boron (B) and manganese (Mn) deficiencies have been noted. Illustrative colour photographs of these deficiencies are given in the Kenya Atlas of Coffee Pests and Diseases (9), Plates 74, 75 (N), 73 (Fe), 72 (Mn), 78 (Zn) and 79, 80, 81, 82 and 83 (B).

Plant nutrient additions to coffee in the ROY are made with organic manure applications but also with fine silt and clay carried in the irrigation water and by salts in the irrigation water. The generally high soil pH values are most probably attributable to long term irrigation water application and the uplift of sub-surface water by capillary action with evaporative surface loss in many fine sand and silty sand soils. Stone mulching will reduce the tendency for upward salt movement in the soil profile. In general inorganic fertilisers are not applied to coffee at the present time.

Key to Mineral Deficiency or Imbalance Symptoms

When mineral elements which are essential to the nutrition of the coffee tree are in short supply or are not in balance with other elements taken up by the tree, the foliage develops certain definite symptoms i,e, colours and/or patterns, indicative of the deficiency syndrome. It is not possible to indicate the detailed differences between these symptoms clearly by description.

Key to Plant Nutrient Deficiency/Imbalance Symptoms of Arabica Coffee

A. *Symptoms starting on new, young growth*   *Nutrient/Deficient*

    I. Leaves of uniform colour over entire area:
    (a) Leaf production and growth reduced
- Young leaves are uniform pale green to yellow colour. Total leaf production reduced; in severe cases size of leaf and branch internode length may also be reduced.   *Nitrogen*

    (b) No reduction in lead production and growth apparent
- Terminal 1 or 2 leaf pairs pale olive-green (may show a reticulate appearance over leaf surface) to bright lemon-yellow with abrupt transition to normal healthy green leaf colour in neighbouring leaf pair.   *Manganese*

    II. Leaves showing a pattern with midrib and veins darker than the tissue between the veins:
    (a) Leaf size and growth reduced
- Leaves very reduced in size, narrow and pointed; main and lateral leaf veins green contrasting with pale green-yellow tissue between veins; branch internode distance very short producing a leaf rosette appearance. Cherry size greatly reduced in severe conditions.   *Zinc*

    (b) Leaves apparently normal in shape and size
- Terminal leaves with a rather coarse chlorotic mottle; margin between main veins (green) and pale green to yellow tissue between veins is not clearly defined. At a distance rather similar to nitrogen deficiency.   *Sulphur*

- Fine network of green veins on a very light green to yellow background. General rate of growth may be reduced. In very severe cases leaves may be almost white to very pale yellow with brown edges and complete death of leaves and dieback of branch tip may occur.   *Iron*

III. Other Symptoms of new young growth:
- Distal (tip) portion of leaf becomes pale olive-green in colour, proximal portion of leaf remains a healthy, dark green colour. In severe cases terminal bud dies followed by multiple branching at the node (or at an older node if there is branch dieback also) to produce a 'fanning' effect not unlike insect damage. In some cases the whole top of a multiple stem tree may die off in this way e.g. parts of Southern Highland Province.   *Boron*

B. *Symptoms starting on mature leaves frequently associated with crop production*

I. Fading of chlorophyll starting in localised areas and gradually spreading:
- Chlorophyll fades in patches along margins of distal leaf edge rapidly turning brown. Patches join up to form eventually a brown margin of irregular width on leaf edges. (This syndrome should not be confused with salinity damage in coffee which is very similar.)   *Potassium*

- Fading of chlorophyll starts in blade of leaf parallel to the midrib and slowly moves outwards between the main veins. The tissue near the base of the leaf on either side of the midrib frequently remains green in the shape of an inverted V. The pattern has been described as a coarse herring-bone type of chlorosis. Colour change of fading tissue is from healthy green through pale olive-green to yellow and finally bronze.   *Magnesium*

- Fading of the chlorophyll starts along the leaf edges and slowly moves inwards in an irregular manner.   *Calcium*

II. Fading of chlorophyll lot localised:

- All leaves on a bearing branch gradually fare through dull green to olive-green to yellow as crop matures; leaves exposed to sunshine change colour more quickly to a greater extreme than leaves or parts thereof which are self-shaded. The colour change occurs in hot dry weather during the later stages of crop maturation.   *Nitrogen*

- Patches of lemon-yellow colour develop on the old leaves and may change to red-bronze (Autumn tint). Sometimes whole leaves change colour in this manner. Younger leaves may show a dark blue-green colouration (in absence of tree shade) and hang in a characteristic manner from the branch i.e. downwards and backwards. The condition is often associated with periods of drought i.e. dry soil conditions, either in the presence or absence of crop and may also be brought on by prolonged periods of temporarily waterlogged soil conditions, particularly when there is a general tendency for active growth to take place at the same time. Note that an attack of ring borer (see Figure 11) will often produce these leaf symptoms.   *Phosphorus*

III Other conditions of old leaves:

- In areas where manganese deficiency is known to occur seasonally (refer section A.I.b.) old leaves on branches may show a coarse rather diffuse chlorotic mottle with the leaf veins standing out in a darker green colour than the surrounding leaf tissue. This may be pale green or pale yellow. The chlorotic mottle is more diffuse than it is when iron is deficient.   *Manganese*

  There are a further series of symptoms associated with boron deficiency (refer section A.III) which may or may not occur together. These are: (a) Corking along the midrib on the underside of the coffee leaf due to it splitting; (b) The production of long narrow, leathery textured leaves on a branch; (c) The production of abnormal shaped, malformed   *Boron* coffee leaves i.e. bifurcated midrib or half-leaves which look as though the top half has been pulled off.

It must be emphasised that the accurate diagnosis of nutritional upsets in coffee is a skilled task.

Organic Manure

The usual form of mineral nutrient application to coffee is dry, often fine, organic manure. It is best applied to the trees before the main rainy season is expected (in late March to April), during January, February and early March.

It should be applied to the *sahani* soil surface spread in a circle extending from 10 - 15 cm away from the coffee stem outwards to the edge of the drip circle. It should be lightly worked into the topsoil. The stone mulch should be removed for this operation and replaced after the manure application.

It is much less effective to bury organic matter and manure in a pit on one side of the tree since this supplies only a part of the root system. Since movement upwards in the tree is spiral not all of the primary branches will receive a fair supply of the additional minerals. Furthermore, there will be no beneficial effect of the organic matter in the coffee topsoil i.e. structure improvement, enhanced nutrient and moisture holding capacities, for the benefit of the whole of feeder root system particularly where a stone mulch is present. Organic manure should never be placed in a heap around and against the coffee stem. This is bad for the stem and is not a good position for access by the feeding roots.

Average annual dressings should be of the order of:

Tree Age in the Field (Years)	Kg/Tree of Manure
1 - 3	3 - 4
4 - 5	4 - 6
> 5	6 - 9

Fertilisers

The best form of fertiliser to apply for nitrogen input to the ROY coffee would be ammonium sulphate because it has a strong acidifying effect on the soil and thus would improve iron nutrition. However the import cost per unit of nitrogen is high in comparison with urea fertiliser which contains a little more than twice the unit nitrogen content. Therefore, it will not be so beneficial as ammonium sulphate at equal rates of nitrogen application.

If fertiliser nitrogen is used it should be applied in one or two dressings depending upon the rate per hectare. The first application is made at the end of March to April after the rains have arrived; a second application would be made in the middle to end of July. It should be broadcast in the *sahani* in the same manner as the organic manure.

It is possible that compound NPK fertiliser may eventually be used. The application rates could be related to the nitrogen content but the ratio of $N:P_2O_5:K_2O$ in the compound fertiliser will be significant. Unless potassium deficiency is diagnosed, the ratio should be of the order of 2 - 4:1:1 - 2, $N:P_2O_5:K_2O$ or high nitrogen, low phosphorus, low to medium potassium. Timing of the application will be the same as for the straight fertiliser. Where potassium deficiency is confirmed or foliar diagnosis reveals seasonal shortages, the compound fertiliser ratio should be 4:1:4, $N:P_2O_5:K_2O$.

The rates of nitrogen to be applied will vary with tree age; indicative levels can only be given in the absence of field trial studies.

Tree Age in the Field	Fertiliser-N/ha	
(years)	(Kg)	Frequency of Application
1 - 2	20	1
3 - 6	40	2
7 +	60 - 80	2

Iron chlorosis which adversely affects both green bean and liquor quality (13) may be controlled with ground applications of an iron chelate (20 - 40 kg/ha) but this treatment is expensive and rather erratic in both the beneficial effect and degree of persistence. (n.b. The permanent, long-term control is to lower soil pH levels to 6.2 or less with regular use of ammonium sulphate fertiliser plus soil dressing with sulphur). Some control is obtained by spray nutrient application and this is also the method recommended for controlling Zn, B and Mn deficiencies when these are diagnosed. However, as with fertiliser use, economic returns to expensive ground or nutrient spray treatments is dependent upon good basic coffee husbandry in the first place.

The spray nutrient treatment will need to consist of 3-4 spray applications/ season, one of which should be made in June during the break in the wet season. Treatment could be with Fertilon Combi Red at the rate and volume recommended for citrus crops. If an iron (Fe) control treatment alone is to be applied a proprietary iron chelate spray material may be used and may be less expensive than Fertilon Combi Red. Rates of FeHEEDTA or FeDTPA chelates suggested have been 1 - 2 kg/420 l as a spray or 10 - 50 g of solid chelate per tree watered into the soil. Repeated spraying each season is necessary to maintain any degree of control of Fe, Zn, B and Mn deficiency conditions whereas ground application of ipn chelate may have a more persistent effect.

11. PHYSIOLOGICAL AND OTHER DISORDERS

A number of physiological conditions and other disorders occur in the ROY coffee but the commonest and most serious is overbearing with consequential development of a biennial or triennial cropping pattern.

Genetic Effects

Variegation or Marbling: leaves are seen with strongly contrasting dark green and light yellow areas on a branch. The variegated areas on the leaf are quite irregular and follow no particular pattern. Sometimes only a few leaves on a branch are affected but sometimes it is all the leaves. (8), Figure 1 and (9), Plate 64 illustrate this condition in detail.

The condition is inherent in the genetic make-up of the tree and can be passed on by striking cuttings of the affected portion. It may be carried in a proportion of the seed from such branches and variegated trees make spectacular ornamental plants. Elimination of the affected part(s) of the tree may be done by pruning them off.

Fasciation: This is a condition of new sucker growth which occurs with rapid regeneration after trees have been heavily cut back. The new sucker growth produces a fan shaped growth of tightly packed, joined together, flattened stems and leaves. Removal of affected sucker growth is advised and the condition is illustrated in (8), Figure 2.

Climatic Effects

Hail Damage: physical damage to the coffee leaves consists of shredding and tearing; branches are severely bruised and each bruise later becomes a deep scar, generally elongated along the stem. Cherry may be knocked off the tree or may be bruised on one side and the damaged bean may fail to develop. Damage is illustrated in (8), Figure 3.

Lightning Damage: electrical discharge by lightning may kill coffee trees but damage varies in degree from complete destruction to slight scorching. Shaded coffee is less susceptible.

In unshaded coffee a patch of trees will be affected; a few trees in the centre may be killed while surrounding trees will show some dieback on the upper branches, resembling drought symptoms. A diagnostic feature of lightning damage is a reddish-brown discolouration of the outer layer of living wood tissue (the cambium underneath the bark) which is seen when the bark is stripped away within a short time of the damage occurring. External tree damage shows up about 10 days after the lightning has struck.

In shaded coffee a shade tree may be killed or damaged and the roots of surrounding coffee trees may also be damaged. Damage to the tree and to the cambium is illustrated in (9), Plate 57.

Sun Scorch: this condition can occur on both leaf and cherry (see (9), Plates 60 and 61). It occurs on leaves of young coffee seedlings not quite hardened off in the nursery, after field planting in sunny conditions with no shade cover. It may occur on leaf and cherry following shade tree pruning or hard coffee pruning. Apparently leaves (or cherry) growing in heavily shaded conditions cannot adapt to and withstand sudden exposure to direct sunlight. The cherry scorch is usually associated with water shortage in the tree.

Cherry is usually most susceptible in the latter part of the maturation period during a drought situation or when there is a shortage of leaf due to exposure or overbearing and consequent leaf loss (refer to later section on overbearing in this Chapter). Cherry that is maturing yellow-ripe (overbearing situation) rather than red-ripe is particularly susceptible. The condition can be quite serious.

Wind Damage: arabica coffee will not tolerate exposure to a persistent wind. The windward side of the tree is thin, ragged, and the primary growth is shortened compared with the leeward side. Leaves may be distorted and broken with necrotic marks on the margin. Viewed from the side, affected trees are lopsided and uneven.

Hot and Cold: this condition is common in high altitude coffee or areas with hot and cold nights giving a wide diurnal temperature range, when the coffee is not adequately shaded and sheltered. It may occur to such an extent that tree growth is severely stunted and this is particularly the case in new coffee plantings. Young coffee affected in this way may take several years to recover if there is no attempt to introduce or increase shade and shelter from cold winds and temperatures.

Symptoms on the leaves are described as: leaves commonly small and leathery, have a very uneven yellow band at the margin which is broader near the leaf tip (10). With severe symptoms the yellow margin extends within the area between the leaf veins and only a small part of the leaf remains green. At a later stage the yellow margin may die back and the tissue turn brown. These symptoms occur in exposed leaves, usually on the upper part of a tree; self-shaded, unexposed leaves are free of symptoms as are leaves near the ground level. The condition is illustrated in (8), Figure 4; (9) Plate 59 in detail.

Intermittent Chlorosis: a condition associated with extremely cold short-term conditions e.g. one or two very cold nights. All the leaves of the same age (often over a considerable number of trees) are completely yellow while older leaves and younger leaves produced subsequently are a normal green colour. In some cases isolated green spots of varying size, pattern and density are visible on the yellow leaf surface. The condition may be of general or quite local occurrence in coffee trees in a small hollow (10). It does not generally occur in shaded coffee. The condition is illustrated in (8), Figure 5; (9), Plate 65 in detail.

Drought: in the absence of sufficient available soil moisture in hot dry weather a coffee tree will wilt i.e. the leaves lose their turgor or rigidity and hang limp and flaccid. Wilting is due to insufficient water being taken up by the roots to replace the water that is lost from the leaf surface. If the condition is not too severe and even though it may occur daily during the hottest part of the day, the leaves recover. If the water shortage is too severe the wilt is irreversible; under these conditions part or all of the leaves and stems may die and both leaf and stem will turn brown. Sometimes only the leaves on the tips of the branches turn brown and die. With the onset of rain or the application of irrigation water the remainder of the leaves and stems will return to normal health leaving tip-leaf death. See Plates 26 and 27; (9), Plate 56.

Crinkle Leaf: symptoms of this condition may be confused with the Hot and Cold symptoms on cropping coffee. This is a puzzling condition which is not controlled by insecticides or nutrient sprays but has responded in East Africa to one fungicide (Captan) though not at economic control rates.

Symptoms have been described (10) as a diagnostic small brown lesion which makes its appearance on very young leaves usually well before they are unfolded in the bud. Corkiness of the veins and interveinal areas occurs, sometimes there are shortened internodes but the typical final symptom is a sickle-shaped leaf though various other patterns of leaf deformation can occur including almost complete destruction of the leaf blades. Refer to illustrations in (8) Figure 7 and (9) Plate 58. This does not seem to be a major problem in the ROY nor is it one that has been definitively associated with climatic conditions.

Senescence Chlorosis: when coffee leaves reach the end of their natural life undamaged by insect pest, disease or physiological condition they develop a characteristic chlorosis pattern just prior to leaf fall. The midrib, lateral veins and to a lesser or greater degree the fine leaf veins, turn bright yellow and contrast strongly with the green leaf blade colour between the veins. This is illustrated in (9), Plate 63.

Overbearing Dieback amd Debility Syndrome

This is a problem of major significance in the ROY. The term overbearing is with respect to actual yield/unit area or yield/tree, a relative one. The symptoms and the aftermath in later seasons can develop over a wide range of yield levels depending upon the strength and condition of the tree.

Overbearing develops in the latter part of the crop maturation period when there is an adverse leaf:crop ratio i.e. when there is too little leaf (number and area) to support the crop that sets to a normal red-ripe maturity.

The symptoms are:
i) the shedding of older leaves from the main bearing primary branches.
ii) colour changes of the young leaves on heavily cropping branches; green-pale green - yellow-bright yellow.
iii) the bright yellow leaves may scorch to a brown colour and fall off or they may also fall off without scorching.
iv) the branch begins to die back from the tip.
v) the crop on the branch ripens to a yellow and not a red maturation colour but may have a faint pink tinge. In extreme cases the cherries may dry and turn black, dying on the branch. The yellow cherry is very subject to sun scorch.
vi) the quality of the coffee bean from the yellow-ripe cherry is poor and there will be small bean size; in the blackened cherry there may be little or no bean at all.
vii) death of feeder roots and even feeder root bearers and storage roots in the soil as carbohydrates are removed to support the crop.
viii) sometimes where there is a later flowering the smaller green cherries turn black and are shed without filling. This is sometimes referred to as "squeeze" and can occur on both overbearing trees and on apparently healthy trees that produce a small late crop in the presence of an older main crop of cherry. It is a physiological self - regulating crop control measure triggered by the tree in response to adverse conditions (refer to (9), Plate 67).

Causes of the condition are an adverse leaf:crop ratio due to any one or a combination of the following factors:
i) heavy leaf fall during the crop season due to pest or disease attack.
ii) lack of pruning or under-pruning at the beginning of the coffee season so that too heavy a crop is allowed to set.
iii) a weak root system.
iv) drought conditions during crop maturation.
v) lack of available soil nitrogen (absolute and/or due to dry soil conditions).

Nitrogen shortage limits the production of carbohydrates in the leaf and the quantity available for crop development, for sustaining the root system and for storage in the root system. The crop is the primary "sink" for carbohydrate as the bean matures; if the leaves cannot meet the demands it is withdrawn from the roots. These then die back followed by the leaf colour changes, leaf fall, scorching and terminal primary branch death referred to above.

If the onset of the condition is detected in the very early stages young crop may be stripped off the heavy cropping branches, 1/3 - 2/3 of it, taking care not to remove any leaves. This should prevent branch dieback and so preserve the cropping potential for the following season. If branch tips die back there will be no crop on them in the following season. If secondary/tertiary branches grow out there may be some crop in the second season. However, if a whole primary branch dies that is the end of its cropping life. Thus, these conditions impose either a biennial or a triennial bearing rhythm, and average annual yields are substantially reduced. The effect of overbearing on theoretical yields of green bean per tree are illustrated in the following table.

Mature Coffee Trees (Kg Green Bean per Tree)		
Time	**Unpruned & Overbearing***	**Pruned and not Overbearing**
Year 1	0.50	0.35
Year 2	0.03	0.27
Year 3	0.35	0.28
Year 4	0.09	0.36
Total	0.97	1.26

(*biennial bearing)

Over the four years the regular bearing healthy coffee produced 22% more crop spread more evenly between the years. This coffee would be of a very much better quality.

Trees that have been seriously weakened by overbearing are easily detected because of the debility syndrome or characteristic tree condition; both old and young trees are equally susceptible. Such trees have a "waisted" appearance, a thick dense leafy skirt area with very low production potential unless 'opened up' to the light, a "thin" or "waisted" middle tree section of dead or partially dead and dying, leafless primary branches with no crop potential for at least one season. Above this middle section is a short tuft of shortened, leafy primaries at the top of the vertical stems, on the older branches of which a small crop may be carried. Often this also overbears in the season following the mid-tree section overbearing.

Following mid-section overbearing there is profuse weak leaf and branch growth in this part of the tree when tree growth recommences. The description of this growth has been detailed (14) and illustrated (8), Plates 6A and 6B. Briefly there will be large or small leaves with yellow margins, iron and/or zinc deficiency leaf symptoms, leaves may be puckered, twisted, wrinkled or otherwise distorted, with shortened internodes at the branch tip and there may be some large, flabby (soft) leaves at the end of a branch exhibiting iron chlorosis. The production of large leaves generally indicates an improvement in growth conditions.

The overbearing syndrome is illustrated in (9), Plate 62, and here in Plates 28, 29, 30 and 31.

Pruning a tree correctly after overbearing is a special problem. The usual pruning time is as soon after harvesting is completed as possible. Not so for overbearing trees. They should be left alone to recover as best they can until just before the rains are expected or following the first pre-wet season irrigation (refer Chapter 9). It is then necessary to:

i) thin out the dense, bushy, green leaved skirt section to let light in. This requires removing all secondary growth for 15 cm along primary branches, from the vertical stem. Remove all upward and downward growing secondary branches and if necessary reduce primary pairs (arising from one node) to one on alternate sides of the primary branch moving outwards from the vertical stem.

ii) cut off all dead primary branch wood in the mid-section. This may be whole primaries that are dead or only part of them. Clear out secondary growth near to the vertical stem if it is very dense and profuse.

iii) no treatment of the cropping green tufty section at the top of each vertical stem is necessary unless they develop early symptoms of overbearing in the next season. If this happens remove 1/3 - 2/3 of the green cherry but not the leaves.

The alternative pruning approach if the overbearing has been severe and the debility of the tree is serious, is to convert the trees to a new pruning cycle. Half tree pruning or stumping with a 'lung' or 'mama' branch are alternative approaches to the action described above (refer Chapter 6). It is difficult to decide what to do with trees that have been seriously damaged by overbearing. Since root death occurs before branch dieback and is not seen by the grower, seriously affected trees should be given the greatest possible assistance to recover e.g. mulch and manure.

12. DISEASES AND PESTS

Although some diseases and pests do attack coffee in the ROY, the harsh, dry climatic conditions generally prevent widespread, devastating attacks. Locally intense attacks of one or two pests do occur in some regions.

There is a major problem concerned with the application of modern agricultural chemicals to control diseases and pests. While it is not a problem to list modern fungicides or insecticides with proven ability to control specific conditions that have been tested as safe for such use, the safety factor is with respect to the green bean of commerce. In the ROY the dry cherry skins are widely used to prepare a beverage named Gishr but there have been few if any toxic residue analysis studies on cherry skins because they are not generally used in food or drink for human consumption.

If modern agricultural chemicals were to be introduced for general use to control diseases and pests, such studies would be essential.

A further problem in many areas of the ROY will be the ready and easy availability of a clean water supply for spray application of agricultural chemicals unless very low volume (v-l-v) or ultra low volume (u-l-v) application techniques are available.

Diseases

A. *In the Nursery*

Damping Off. The wilting and death of small coffee seedlings usually at the soldier (helmet), butterfly or 1 - 2 true leaf stage is the result of fungal attack on the stem at soil level. Over-wet soil conditions and heavy shade are predisposing to the development of this condition which is caused by various fungi such as *Rhizoctonia solani* or *Pythium* spp. Deaths usually occur in patches of seedlings. Refer to (15), Figure 1 and (9), Plate 50 for illustrations.

Damping off can be prevented from spreading by watering a copper fungicide solution onto the soil (0.5% w/w of a 50% copper fungicide i.e. 5 g/l).

Brown Eye Spot. Principally a disease of the nursery plant. The fungus *Cercospora coffeicola* causes small brown spots on the leaf usually with a reddish brown margin and eventually a grey centre. It causes premature leaf fall.

Brown eye spot attack can be prevented from spreading (the damage at spraying will not be corrected) by spraying the seedling leaves with copper fungicide (0.5% w/w of a 50% copper fungicide i.e. 5 g/l) using a knapsack sprayer and a medium-fine droplet size. With a CP15 or a CP3 knapsack sprayer (see Chapter 7) use a cone nozzle (SA04-520 nozzle holder and cap fitted with spray disc size No. 12, 1.2 mm hole) for general use.

B. In the Field

Brown Eye Spot. Brown eye spot attack does occasionally occur in the field and the most serious attacks are usually on unthrifty coffee trees. An application of manure (or fertiliser nitrogen) with irrigation if the weather is dry, will assist the tree to grow away from the condition. A copper fungicide spray may be applied as previously described for the nursery seedlings. Illustrations will be found in (15), Figure 3 and (9), Plate 43.

Coffee Leaf Rust. Coffee Leaf Rust *(Hemileia vastatrix)* has been noted in the ROY coffee due most probably to the dry climatic conditions, but is not a major problem. In the unlikely event that night time application of irrigation water through an overhead system was practised this disease could become very damaging. Illustrations in (15), Figure 2 and (9), Plates 40 and 41.

Brown Blight of Cherry. This condition is occasionally seen but should not be confused with sun scorch on yellow ripening cherry where drought/overbearing occurs. Only nearly ripe or ripe cherries are attacked. They develop sunken brown spots on the skin caused by the fungus *Colletotrichum coffeanum*. The damage is generally slight though the pulp may adhere to the bean and no direct control measures are normally required. Note that a much more aggressive form of this fungus (var. *virulens*) causes the very serious condition known as Coffee Berry Disease in some African countries e.g. Ethiopia, Kenya, Tanzania. An illustration of brown blight is shown in (9), Plate 46.

Collar Rot. A fungus or several different fungal species can attack the stems of mature coffee trees at soil level effectively ring-barking the tree and killing it completely. A white mycelium is often observed encircling the stem base. It is seen most commonly in irrigated, heavily shaded coffee with soil ± manure heaped against the stems of the coffee trees. The specific fungal agent(s) is not known but will almost certainly originate from the natural soil flora.

Sooty Mould. This is not a parasitic fungus on coffee but grows superficially on the leaves, living on the excretions of certain insects, usually scale insects. The

Diseases and Pests

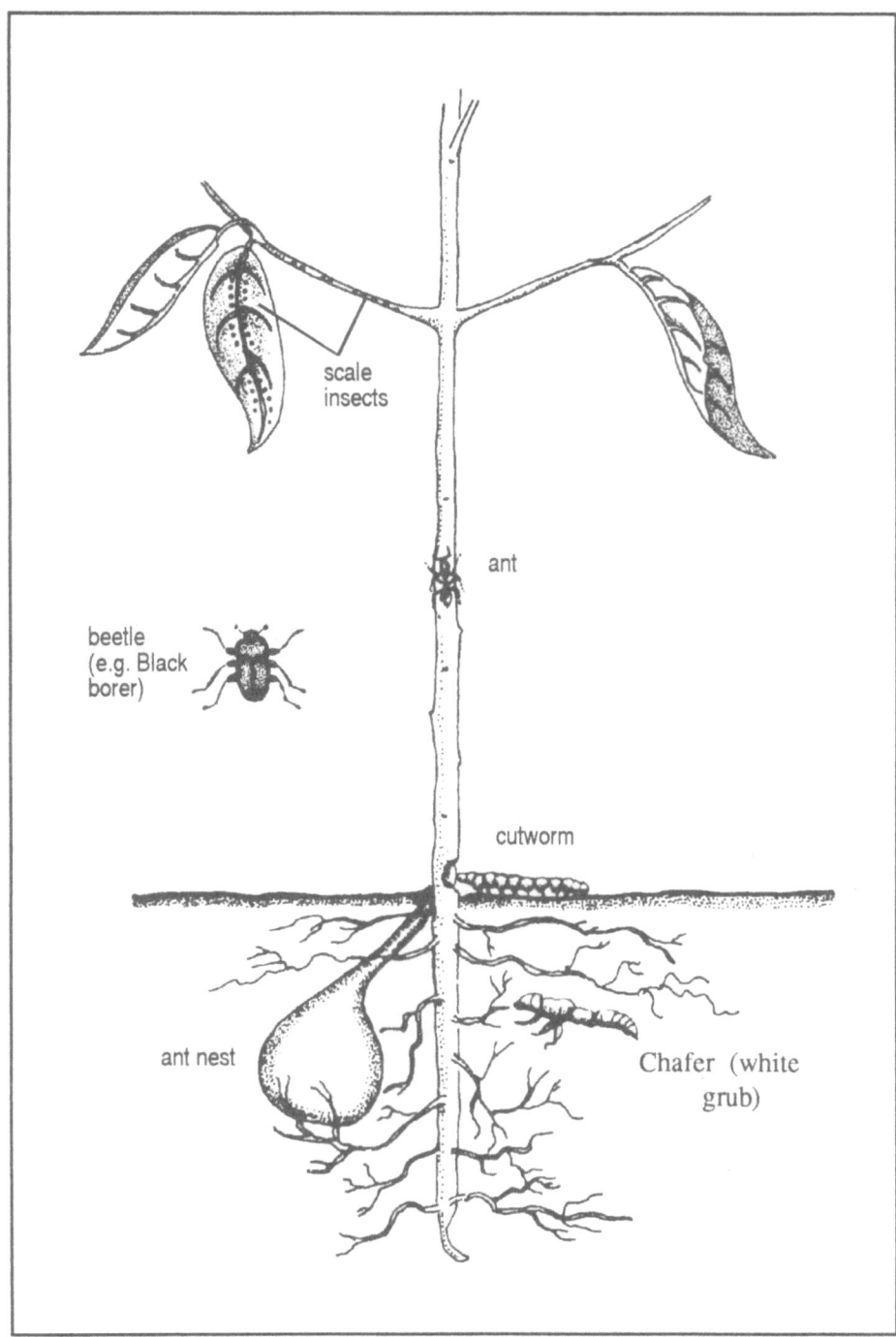

Figure 9: Coffee Pests

black powdery coating easily rubs off but a dense general leaf cover can weaken the tree by cutting off the light (energy) source so necessary for photosynthesis. It is a species of Capnodium fungus. Sometimes the insect excretions upon which the fungus feeds may have originated from a shade tree insect pest and not from a pest (scale) on the coffee tree at all. The exudate falls onto the coffee tree from the shade tree pest above it.

Pests

There are a number of insect pests that occur in the ROY coffee and attacks may sometimes be heavy and therefore serious. The problems of control are:

i) recognition of a serious pest attack early enough to exercise an economic control

ii) with a policy of integrated biological control i.e. the identification of pests and the infestation level, it is necessary to know at what attack levels to apply an insecticidal control programme. At levels less than those defined critically, the attack will be economically sustainable and will decline naturally due to predation or parasitisation of the pest and climatic change with the season. Treatment will depend upon the cropping level and the likely crop loss.

iii) the question of insecticide use on cropping coffee trees with chemicals that although cleared for harmful residues in the beans have probably not been evaluated for the cherry skins which form a valuable part of the crop in the ROY.

The pests occurring in the ROY coffee are considered here in relation to whether they attack the coffee roots, main stems, young branches and leaves or the berries.

Some coffee pests are illustrated in Figure 9. These include the chafer or white grub which eats roots and ants (black or brown) which tend scale pests on the green stems or leaves of young coffee, protecting them from natural enemies in return for the sugary excretion they exude. Some leaf eating beetles are also soil inhabiting but this does not include the Black stemborer.

A. Root Pests

In recent years the **White Grub** *Rutelinae* sp. (Chafer) which is the juvenile stage of a beetle, has become an evident pest. It is white or creamy white in colour with a reddish-brown head, see Plate 32 and Figure 9. It is probably present in lesser or greater numbers at all times but the root damage it causes becomes serious in young coffee or when mature coffee is stressed as for example in times of severe drought or debilitation after overcropping. There is some belief that the pest is related to the use of manure in coffee and it is very possible that the eggs and young grubs do occur in fine, dry organic manure.

Control is very difficult requiring either a soil applied insecticide to be mixed in the soil around the coffee roots or a systemic insecticide known to reach the fine root system where it would be ingested by the grub. Safe chemicals for either treatment in coffee are not known; Aldrin or Dieldrin insecticides are banned internationally but have been used as soil applications under nursery conditions in the past. The rates were Dieldrin 50% wettable powder, 2.5 g/10 l or Aldrin, 40% wettable powder, 3 g/10 l, watered onto the soil with a watering can preferably when the soil is moist to assist distribution to the root zone or well worked into the soil under dry conditions.

Cutworm. This is a grey or black caterpillar (*Euxoa segetum* and others) which lives below the soil surface. They cut off young seedlings at soil level and can ringbark older plants. They too are difficult to control since the previously noted insecticides Dieldrin and Aldrin were banned, see Figure 9.

B. Stem Pests

The most serious of these is the **Black Borer** *(Apate monacha)*; the beetle is almost 2 cm long, shiny black in colour and is particularly prevalent on droughted trees. It bores a hole upwards in the main stem for a short distance but does not breed in coffee. The simplest control is to poke a piece of stiff wire up the tunnel to kill the beetle e.g. a length of bicycle spoke is ideal. An alternative method is to soak a piece of cotton wool or absorbent cloth in a volatile liquid like dry cleaning fluid, petroleum spirit or even kerosene and force it up the tunnel. Where beetles are active 'frasse' (saw dust and excreta) drops to the ground and serves as a guide to detection. The damage caused interferes with translocation within the stem and also weakens the tree physically so that with a heavy crop the stem may break. The pest is well illustrated in (9), Plate 17.

C. Leaf and Branch Pests.

Green Scale *(Coccus viridis)*. This can be a serious pest of nursery seedlings and on young coffee trees for the first two or three years in the field. It is well illustrated on the underside of leaves in (9), Plate 6, but it also attacks green wood and sometimes green cherry as well. Occasionally it may attack older trees but rarely becomes a major pest on these. It reproduces rapidly, is a voracious feeder (sucking the tree sap) and is attended by small ants (black or brown in colour) which tend and protect the scale insect from natural enemies for the benefit to them of the excreted honeydew. Often the honeydew secretion is more than the ants can dispose of and the seedlings or young trees becomes covered with the black sooty mould referred to earlier in this chapter.

Control of the scale is dependent upon control of the attending ants. Often after the ants have been controlled, natural enemies will destroy the scale in time.

The scale insect may be sprayed with white oil emulsion (Alboleum) at a concentration of 31 ml/l. Other controls are with white oil + malathion or with Disytox or Gusathion emulsion (approximately 4.5 - 5 ml/l of 20% emulsifiable concentrate). The quantity of Malathion is 22 ml Malathion M>L> 50% plus 222 ml While Oil and 44 ml of wetting agent ot detergent in 20 l of spray or at the manufacturers recommended rates. None of these sprays will be wholly effective unless the ants are controlled and in the ROY only the use of white oil can be recommended as a safe treatment.

Ants attending the scale may be controlled by spraying or by painting chemical onto the stem(s) of the coffee tree up which they walk. Suitable control in Kenya is obtained with the following:

Sprays:
- Ethion — 20 ml/20 l water
- Dursban — 30 ml/20 ml "
- Decis — 100 ml/20 l "

Stem application (by paint brush, a band 10 cm wide)
- Supracide — 1 l/20 l water
- Ethion — 1 l/20 l "
- Dursban — 0.7 l/20 l "
- Decis — 0.75 l/20 l "
- Inacide Paint — undiluted ground bait
- Amdro — yellow granular bait, broadcast under affected trees (6.7 kg/ha).

(Note this material is soluble in water and breaks down in sunlight so it should be applied to a dry soil in late afternoon.)

White Waxy Scale *(Ceroplastis breviscaudus)* White, immobile insects like blobs of cream or dabs of sugar icing on the branches which usually occur in small numbers but may occur extensively. They are very difficult to control by spraying the white stage on branches but juveniles occurring on leaves can be destroyed. The white waxy blobs may be removed physically or infected branches can be cut off and left on the ground. Generally slow breeding and with natural enemies they do not usually require chemical control. Attendant ants if present, should be controlled as noted under Green Scale above. White oil in water (31 ml/l water) sprayed to run off in the dry season will control juveniles on the undersides of the leaves (but not the white wax covered adults). The adult pest is well illustrated in (9), Plate 8. All the scales are sucking insects feeding on plant sap.

Thrips *(Diarthrothrips coffeae)* do occasionally present a major problem in dry weather with very high daily temperatures i.e. at lower altitudes. They live and feed on the undersides of coffee leaves on mature trees. Damaged leaves become dry, limp and silvery coloured with dark spots of faecal matter on the lower surface. Premature leaf loss then occurs. Chemical control is possible with the same materials that control Leaf Miner i.e. Sumithion, Folithion or Karati sprays.

Leaf Miner *Leucoptera meyricki* (sun loving) and *Leucoptera caffeina* (shade loving). Damaged leaves are shed by the tree prematurely and a serious attack can lead to an overbearing problem because of this leaf loss. Both pest and the damage are well illustrated in reference (9), Plates 23, 24 and 25. Under the system of integrated control practised in Kenya, coffee (combining and integrating chemical and biological - natural enemy - control measures) chemicals are not applied until and unless there are more than 35 of these small moths per tree. The count of moths is made on a small random sample of coffee trees in a coffee plot. In a large area of many plots all coffee owners would need to act together otherwise re-infestation of a treated plot from adjacent untreated coffee plots could occur.

The attack symptoms are irregular brown areas on the top of the coffee leaves. When the brown top skin of the leaf is peeled away from a fresh 'mine', several small white caterpillars are seen. The caterpillars emerge from the mine and pupate in a white cocoon either on the underside of coffee leaves or on the ground. Eventually they change into small white moths, see (9), Plate 25.

Chemical control measures are possible with Fenitrothion (15 ml of 50% miscible liquid, ML, per 20 l water), Fenthion at the same rate, applying about 0.5 l of spray per mature tree. Sumithion or Folithion (10 ml of 50% emulsifiable concentrate per 20 l water) or ICI Karati at the manufacturers recommended rate. Note that these rates of application are based upon field studies in countries outside the ROY and require practical validation under conditions in the ROY.

D. Berry Pests.

Berry Moth *(Prophantis smaragdina)* occurs commonly and can lead to substantial berry loss. Soft green cherries are damaged by small caterpillars which bore into them and eat the inside of the cherry. It emerges and will attack other cherries on the node after spinning a fine web between the cherries on that node.

Damaged cherries turn black but do not fall off the tree. The caterpillars are the juvenile form of a small, inconspicuous yellow and brown coloured moth with a wingspan of about 1.24 cm. Berry moth can only survive on flower buds or young green cherry in which the parchment cover of the beans has not hardened. Reference to (9), Plate 26 illustrates berry moth damage and the caterpillar with silk web.

Control of berry moth must be done early in the season when attacks are likely to occur. Check the trees at and soon after flowering. If flower buds or young cherries are being eaten spray immediately. Once the caterpillar is present in the shelter of the cherry with the additional protection of the silk web and faecal matter it cannot be controlled with standard insecticides. Control of the pest is possible with the chemicals described under the Leaf Miner pest section. Once again in a coffee area with many adjacent plots farmed by different owners or tenants, a coordinated control programme will be necessary where the pest is present generally over the coffee, to prevent re-infestation.

Economic pest control in coffee is a further area that needs applied research study in the ROY. It is an essential part, but only a part, of any improved coffee growing programme.

13. HARVESTING AND PROCESSING

Coffee is grown with the object of producing a good quality bean (size and blue-green colour) and a good quality dried cherry skin from which a fine tasting coffee drink or a quality 'Gishr' are produced respectively. If the field husbandry is satisfactory both these objectives will be achieved by picking ripe coffee cherry, drying it quickly and evenly, storing it well to even out the moisture content, hulling it carefully in a proper machine without undue pressure or heat, either or both of which destroy bean quality, and finally storing the green bean and the hulled skins under clean, dry conditions indoors where there is full shade. All the coffee in the ROY is processed by the dry method.

The quality of coffee (green bean and skins) is only as good as it inherently is when the cherries are picked. Processing harvested crop can only either (a) maintain and retain the potential quality or (b) downgrade or disimprove the quality of the final end product. For example, droughted coffee on the tree will always be droughted whether the final bean is good, bad or indifferent depending upon the processing of it.

Picking

The best quality coffee is obtained from harvests of red ripe cherries. Underripe cherries (green or yellow) or yellow ripe cherries off overbearing trees, over ripe cherries (dark purple, brown or black) or any mixture of these different categories will give inferior quality.

Generally speaking main crop coffee is harvested only 2 - 3 times; for more selective quality, harvesting may require a larger number of picking rounds. The last pick is usually a mixed pick of ripe and unripe cherries and should be treated separately and not bulked with the fully ripe-picked crop.

Wherever visible iron-deficiency chlorosis is present on the leaves of cropping branches even fully ripe cherries will contain a proportion of Amber Beans (13) of low raw, roast and liquor quality.

Drying

Cherry drying should begin the same day as it is harvested in the field. It is not generally good for quality to store it overnight in bags, However, it is not unusual for the final harvest, a mixed pick including a high proportion of green beans, to be stored in a heap to promote a false ripening of the green bean. Storing ripe cherry in bags or heaps for 24-48 hours promotes a rapid fermentation which may adversely affect green bean quality and will reduce the sweetness of the skins.

Barbecue drying of harvested coffee is generally done on the flat rooftop of a house, in full sun. The cherry may be spread out on the cement roof surface on specially made woven mats, on plastic sheets or even on trays. Whichever is used the drying surface must be clean and well away from aromatic spices, herbs or strong smelling sources e.g. kerosene because coffee has the ability to pick up strong odours during drying or storage which may taint the produce. Drying takes from 7 - 15 days depending upon how thick the drying layer is and the weather conditions. It is not generally covered unless it rains.

The drying area will vary in this approximate manner:
1 cherry layer thick - 2 cm - 1 m^2 area - 15 kg cherry
2 cherry layer thick - 4 cm - 1 m^2 area - 30 kg cherry
3 cherry layer thick - 5-6 cm - 1 m^2 area - 40 kg cherry

1 tonne of red cherry will require approximately 34 m^2 of drying area; mats are usually 3 m^2 and the need is for about 12 mats/tonne cherry.

The recommended thickness of the drying layer is 2 - 4 cm and the layers should be thoroughly turned by rake or by hand, twice a day at 11 am and 3 pm approximately. When the thickness of the cherry layer is greater than 5-6 cm and it is not turned frequently every day, drying will be uneven and cherry at the bottom of the layer may begin to rot imparting a poor flavour to both coffee liquor and Gishr.

A dark coloured drying surface e.g. black plastic, is heat absorbing and will assist in evening up the drying between the top and bottom of the cherry layer if the layer is not too thick. Do not dry coffee cherries on a bare soil base though a clean stone or rock surface is satisfactory. Drying on an earth surface can impart off-flavour in the coffee liquor.

In general the drying coffee should be covered at night to protect it from heavy dew or rainfall. If a plastic cover is used this should never rest directly on top of the coffee because there will be condensation of moisture on the underside of the plastic sheet which may re-wet the drying cherry. To ensure adequate circulation of the air raise the plastic cover 20-30 cm above the top of the coffee using a stone or wood support to secure the cover at this height. Where condensation and rewetting of the cherry occurs the drying process is slowed down and a sour flavour will often be detected in the coffee liquor.

As a measure of green bean physical quality, a merchant in Sana'a will receive a typical bulk purchase which contains 5% extraneous matter e.g. stones and 10% broken beans, damage due to an inferior hulling process.

Dry cherry (*bun*) should be stored in heaps or in bags (but not plastic bags/sacks unless they are of a very coarse weave and allow for ventilation) in a fully shaded cool, dry storage place well away from any other strong smelling aromatic sources, kerosene or petroleum spirit etc. Initially, storage like this will allow the coffee to become evenly dried throughout, 9.5 - 11/12%, perhaps 13% moisture content though 9.5 - 11% is the most suitable range.

Hulling

After drying, this is the next most critical stage in processing when the cherry skin, the parchment cover on the beans and a proportion of the silverskin are all separated from the green coffee bean.

Traditionally hulling may be done with a stone mill or by pounding in a pestle and mortar. Both methods produce excessive pressure on the bean which disrupts internal cells and substantially reduces storability. Green bean that is a blotchy green-greyish white in colour is usually a result of excessive hulling pressure with or without too much frictional heat. Some powered sorghum/maize mills have a modification for coffee hulling but these are not commonly available.

The most suitable small scale equipment are hullers specifically made for coffee. The coffee machinery manufacturers make a series of small hullers and John Gordon make two which are hand-operated and one that is power-operated. They are listed below:

- a) John Gordon 'Bukoba' Huller. 9 kg *bun*/hour. Hand-operated
- b) John Gordon No. 10 Africa Huller. 23 kg *bun*/hour. Hand-operated.
- c) John Gordon No.5. Africa Huller. 115 kg *bun*/hour. Power-operated.

These pieces of equipment are adjustable for the size of the *bun* being hulled.

While a period of sound storage of dry cherry (*bun*) after drying is completed will allow an evening out of moisture content, this storage period should not be excessively long i.e. not more than 3 - 6 weeks, before the coffee is hulled. If the *bun* is underdry when hulled, clean hulling is more difficult and damage of the green bean by pressure is more likely.

Roasting

Roasting coffee to a particular stage so that the full flavour potential of the liquor is achieved is not difficult provided elementary preparation of the green bean sample is undertaken. The traditional Mocha coffee liquor so favoured by connoisseurs has a medium body, is acid with a pleasant fruity flavour. Three major harvesting/processing constraints to achieving this desired end are identified as:
- i) the presence of amber beans in many green bean samples.
- ii) the lack of careful grading before roasting
- iii) pressure damage during hulling with rapid and serious bean deterioration in a normally warm, dry atmosphere during storage and transport, prior to roasting.

The first is overcome in some countries by hand-picking or by electronic sorting. The second is an obvious point. If the roasting time and temperature is set for the average bulk of the green bean size (say A grade) then smaller beans e.g. peaberry, will be grossly over-roasted and larger beans e.g. elephant beans, will be under-roasted.

While these matters may not be particularly important for the local market they most certainly are for the export market. For example, none of the several packets of roasted, ground Mocha coffee, vacuum packed, that have been purchased in Sana'a would be classified overseas as good quality Mocha coffee (preparation by the filter method). There is plenty of scope for simple improvements in growing, harvesting and processing the ROY coffee that will result in a high traditional Mocha coffee product.

14. GENERAL OBSERVATIONS

No apology is offered for this chapter of general comment and observation because these are matters that are basic to the continued success and improvement of the national ROY coffee production programme.

Timeliness and the Coffee Calendar

Coffee farmers work on a seasonal basis but where coffee is but one of several crops grown it will need to take its place in the work rota. However, timeliness of operations with coffee is important and for some operations it really is most important. For example, the field planting of coffee seedlings should be done early in a main rainy season. The fact that water for irrigation is available is no reason to undertake a new planting in the dry season or at the end of the wet season. For a variety of sound reasons e.g. atmospheric humidity, cloud cover, incoming radiant energy levels, coffee seedlings will not become established and grow-on so quickly unless given every advantage; this is particularly so for unshaded coffee plantings.

An outline coffee calendar is given in Figure 10. The timing of the operations listed are related to the rainfall distribution pattern and to the harvesting period shown. Obviously the timing and to some degree the distribution of the rainfall season will vary somewhat throughout the ROY but a basic 5 - 6 month wet season with a dry break in the middle, and a 5 - 6 month dry season is general. By adjusting the rainfall distribution pattern and main harvesting period for a particular area, a modified calendar appropriate to that specific area can be drawn up. It should be of basic value to any coffee advisory service and to progressive master farmers.

Irrigation Pattern and Water Use

To get the greatest return per unit of water applied to cropping coffee requires a defined programme that takes into account growth periods, required main flowering time(s), cherry filling and tree survival. Furthermore, the minimum effective volume of water per tree should be applied to the soil surface area below which the main bulk of the active root system exists. These objectives can only be achieved with the greatest economic return to the grower where an effective soil surface mulch is present (organic or inert stone) to reduce evaporative loss etc. The basic system recommended in Chapter 9 is supplemental to the natural rains plus minimal survival treatment.

Root System Development and Early Cropping Levels

This is an area of very great farmer demonstration/instruction need because it involves good seedlings, good planting, good pruning with crop control. The development of an extensive and strong root system during the first 5 years or so in the field is absolutely basic to any regular achievement of the genetic yield potential of the coffee tree. Very heavy cropping, often with overbearing plus root dieback, in field years 3, 4 and/or 5 temporarily delays development and may damage the root system permanently. The more adverse are the environmental conditions the more likely is this to happen and the greater is the need for care and attention to avoid it.

Pest Control

The government coffee staff and many coffee farmers are very keen to have quick and effective pest control chemicals to hand. The general problem of available supplies of clean water in the dry season, the need to test vlv and ulv spray techniques (very low volume and ultra low volume) for the medium term and currently concern about the safety of chemical usage in coffee because the cherry skins may retain toxic residues that persist into the Gishr prepared from them, all emphasise the need for studies appropriate to the problems. With strong national universities present it should be possible to harness post-graduate research potential for the mutual benefit of the researcher and the national needs. Indeed many governments in forward moving countries put great emphasis on this type of university effort for the national good, often to the extent of financial support. This could be raised from coffee revenues and so be used for the benefit of future knowledge to improve the industry.

General Observations

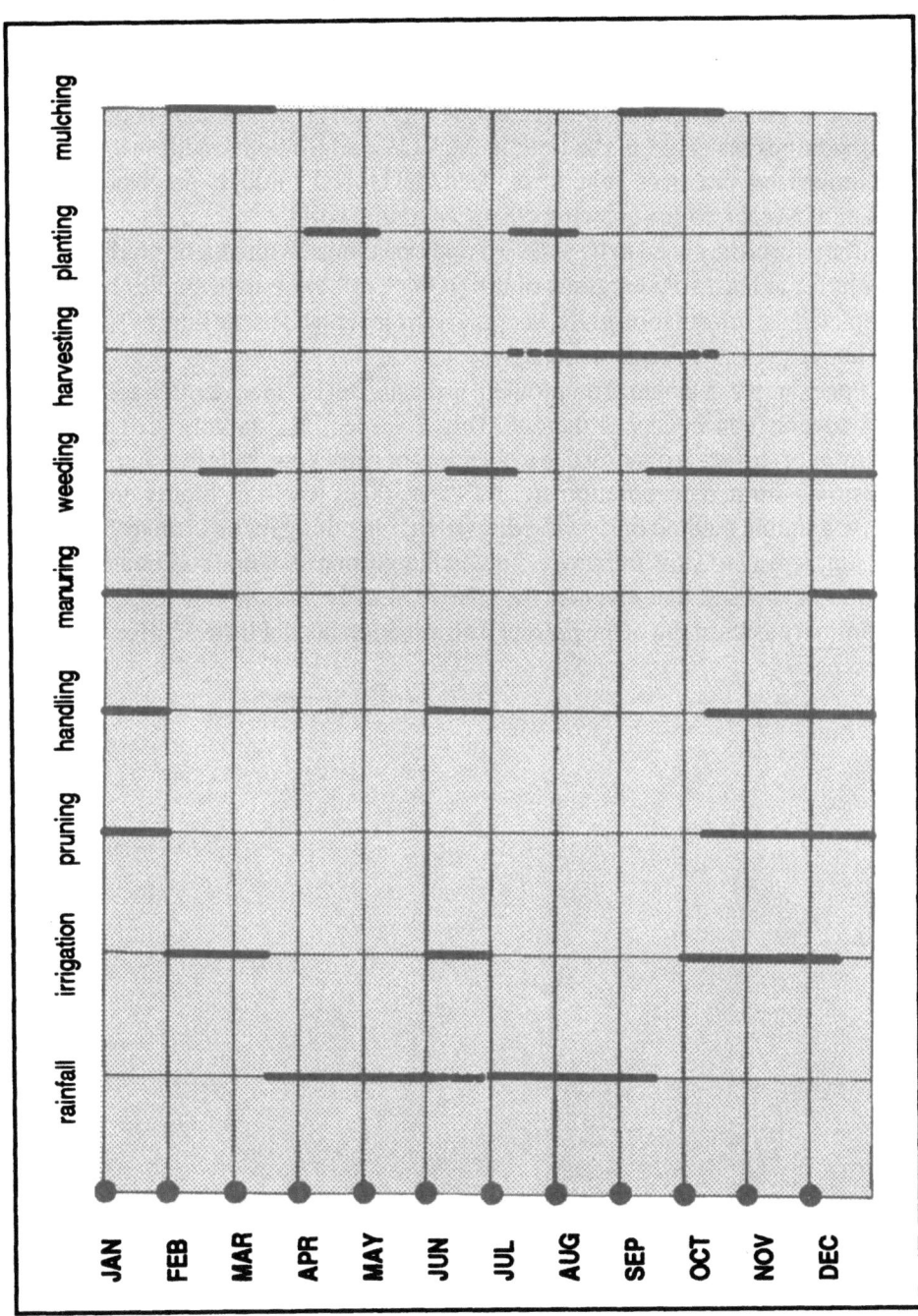

Figure 10: Outline Coffee Calendar

Coffee Research

The husbandry methods and techniques outlined in this manual are based upon (a) conditions observed in the field in the ROY and (b) both traditional practices and improved practices that have been developed through practical applied research in other coffee growing countries of the world.

Therefore, they need to be assessed and can almost assuredly be modified with benefit for at least some regions of the ROY. Until these field studies have been completed the information given here is a basis for considerable improvement over and above present general standards.

For example, a longer term problem is the high pH of many coffee soils and the very adverse consequences thereof. This, I suspect, has largely arisen through centuries of surface irrigation due to a variety of causes e.g. salts in water, capillary and strong surface evaporation etc. At some stages it will be highly desirable to advise a simple method of slowing down or halting this general change. Mulching is a simple way to slow the process down but ultimately some soil treatment will need to be devised that reverses the change already brought about. Of course, a preliminary assessment of the present soils situation in established coffee areas will be necessary.

REFERENCES

1. Wrigley, G., 1988. Coffee, 1-15. London, Longman Scientific and Technical, pp. 639.
2. Rothfos, B., 1985. Coffee Production. 2nd Ed. Hamburg, Gordian-M-R, pp. 366.
3. Fernie, L.M., 1964. Description of the Coffee Tree, Varieties and Selections, 1-8. *In*: Robinson J.B.D. , ed. A Handbook on Arabica Coffee in Tanganyika. Tanganyika Tanzania Coffee Board, pp. 182.
4. Bull, R.A., 1963. Studies on the Effect of Mulch and Irrigation on Root and Stem Development in *Coffea arabica* L. Part 1: Changes in the root system induced by mulching and irrigation. Turrialba, 13(2), 96-115.
5. Robinson, J.B.D., 1986. Tabular Description of Crops Grown in the Tropics. Arabica Coffee (*Coffea arabica* L.). Tech. Memo. 86/5. C.S.I.R.O. Inst. Biol. Scis., Canberra, Australia, pp. 53.
6. IPG/GTZ. Yemen Arab Republic Report 1984.
7. FAO Report 1975. Coffee in Yemen.
8. Riley, E.A., Tapley, R.G., Robinson, J.B.D. and Burdekin, D.A. 1964. Physiological, Nutritional and Other Disorders. 174-182. *In*: Robinson, J.B.D. ed. A Handbook on Arabica Coffee in Tanganyika. Tanganyika (Tanzania) Coffee Board, pp. 182.
9. C.R.S. Staff Kenya, 1961. An Atlas (in colour) of Coffee Pests and Diseases. Plate Nos. 58, 59 and 65.
10. Wormer, T.M. and Firman, I.D. 1961. "Hot and Cold/Debility Symptoms". Kenya Coffee, 1961. 26, 13.
11. Robinson, J.B.D., 1984. A Practical Guide to Growing Arabica and Robusta Coffees in Papua New Guinea. Agricultural Bank of Papua New Guinea, pp. 101.
12. Mwangi, C.N. (ed.) 1983. Coffee Growers Hand-Book 2nd Edition, pp. 128.
13. Robinson, J.B.D., 1960. Amber Beans. Kenya Coffee, 23(2), 91-95.
14. Robinson, J.B.D. and Bull, R.A., 1961. Debility Growth in Coffee. Kenya Coffee, 26, 251.
15. Riley, E.A. and Burdekin, D.A., 1964. Coffee Diseases. In Robinson, J.B.D. ed. A Handbook on Arabica Coffee in Tanganyika. Tanganyika (Tanzania) Coffee Board. pp. 182.

1. Seedlings in a (good) farmers nursery. About 4 - 5 true leaf pair stage. Seedlings too close together and leaf size is small. Some iron chlorosis present.

2. Farmer grown seedlings purchased for planting. Seedlings are weak, etiolated, with iron chlorotic leaves and very weak root systems. Generally of poor quality (compare with Plate 7).

3. Coffee germination bed. Poor practices are a sunken bed rather than a raised bed, randomly broadcast seed with poor, irregular spacing and unhealthy leaf chlorosis symptoms.

4. Nursery seedlings with a complex of nitrogen, iron, zinc and boron deficiencies.

5. Transplanted polypot seedlings showing eventual production of a large (normal) sized leaf pair at the top of the seedling. Note also sporadic iron chlorosis and probable nitrogen shortage symptoms.

6. Stages of growth of seedlings from a germination bed. From left to right the "Helmet", the "Butterfly" and 2 and 3 leaf pair stages. Transplanting to polypots should be made at the "Helmet" or "Butterfly" stages and not later because of potential root damage.

7. Polypot seedlings transplanted. Note early small size of leaf pairs and short internode length. Older seedlings have more normal sized leaf pair (youngest) after growing out of adverse conditions. Note in all cases root damage at time of transplanting.

8. Polypots only half to two thirds full of potting mixture which has been washed out of the pots when watering with a jet at too great a pressure. Low pressure, rose-head watering (sprinkling) is essential.

9. Stone shelter/shade of newly planted coffee seedling.

10. Jebal Numan area. Watering a young coffee seedling that is stone shaded and stone mulched.

11. Demonstrating stone mulching of the tree sahani.

12. Stone mulching of a tree sahani.

13. Six-year old Adeni coffee tree.

14. Young Daiwary coffee tree.

15. Young Shabraque coffee tree.

16. Four-year old Benan coffee tree.

17. Lack of leaf following early cropping on young trees. Note stone mulch.

18. Lack of leaf following early cropping on three year old Burai coffee.

19. Fifteen year old Burai coffee tree with an excess of seven verticals.

20. Coffee tree said to be at least 200 years old with many weak verticals.

21. Tall, weak, whippy overgrown coffee seedling.

22. Demonstrating the bending (Agobiada) system on a weak young coffee tree.

23. Well grown young coffee seedling ready for capping to produce two vertical heads in the first cycle.

24. Mature (30 year old) unpruned coffee under heavy shade.

25. *Stone mulching of coffee terraces, Jebal Numan area.*

26. *Death of coffee trees due to drought.*

27. Coffee trees dying from drought.

28. Overbearing on mature coffee tree. Note yellow-ripe cherry, leaf loss on primary branch and yellow terminal leaves.

29. Early stages of overbearing. Note leaf loss and yellow leaf colour on bearing primaries.

30. Debility after overbearing. Note green leafy skirt, leafless primary branches and green leaved tuft with green cherry moving into overbearing again.

31. Young coffee after overbearing. Note bushy skirt, thin middle and tufty top. Trees are now weak. Coffee is stone mulched.

32. White grubs excavated from beneath a coffee tree.

Bei Fragen zur Produktsicherheit wenden Sie sich bitte an:
If you have any questions regarding product safety,
please contact:

Walter de Gruyter GmbH
Genthiner Straße 13
10785 Berlin
productsafety@degruyterbrill.com